Lurania A. H. Munday

Acacian Lyrics and Miscellaneous Poems

Lurania A. H. Munday

Acacian Lyrics and Miscellaneous Poems

ISBN/EAN: 9783744794886

Printed in Europe, USA, Canada, Australia, Japan

Cover: Foto ©Thomas Meinert / pixelio.de

More available books at **www.hansebooks.com**

Acacian Lyrics

AND

MISCELLANEOUS POEMS.

BY

LURANIA A. H. MUNDAY.

> They tell but dreams—a lonely spirit's dreams—
> Yet ever through their fleeting imagery
> Wanders a vein of melancholy love,
> An aimless thought of home:—as in the song
> Of the caged sky-lark ye may deem there dwells
> A passionate memory of blue skies and flowers,
> And living streams—far off!—Mrs. HEMANS.

CINCINNATI:
APPLEGATE & CO., PUBLISHERS, 43 MAIN STREET.
1861.

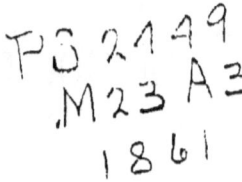

Entered according to the act of Congress, in the year 1857,
By L. A. H. MUNDAY,
In the Clerk's Office of the District Court of the United States for the District of Missouri.

PREFACE.

It is not the mode—literary—to place a work before the public without a few prefatory remarks, either explanatory or apologetical, but feeling conscious that these would avail nothing, I have none to offer.

To those disposed to destroy the fair "net-work" of the mind's temple I have no response. With the generous mind no extenuating voice is needed to plead for those who toil and strive after all that is beautiful, good and true.

Not wishing to presume above its merits, I send forth the present volume, as a bird with untried wings, to the vast world of mind, and if, in the pure realm of thought, there are any to whom its wild warblings afford one draught of intellectual pleasure, or from the stern realities of life beguile a tedious hour—if, in its untutored songs, there is any thing worthy the acceptance and approbation of the refined and good, or waken in pure minds high unities of thought, and soul, my purpose is achieved, my object won.

L. A. H. MUNDAY.

MEMOIRS OF MRS. L. A. H. MUNDAY.

LURANIA A. H. MUNDAY was born April 19th, 1828, in the city of Cincinnati. Her father, who was engaged in the mercantile business, at the time of her birth, shortly after that period, moved to a small country place, located near Mason, Warren County, Ohio, where the subject of these brief memoirs spent most of her childhood's days.

Being of a sensitive and shrinking disposition, she attended the District School but seldom, but grew up in quiet and seclusion, apart from the companionship of children, except that of her brothers, who were younger than herself, under the instruction of her mother. LURANIA was a thoughtful, dreamy child, who chose the most solitary nooks along the streams for her play-ground, and the bright blue violets for her playmates, while again she would apostrophise the stars in childish wonder, questioning what they were, and what their final destiny.

Purity in language, sentiment and manners, were her peculiar characteristics, from her earliest childhood, hence the repugnance and utter disgust, which she felt when brought in contact with coarseness and vulgarity, which was rendered doubly painful from the fact that circumstances over which she had no control, made it impossible to choose such society as would have been congenial to her ardent mind, such as would have fed and nourished her hungry intellect, longing for a full development of the powers of her mind—longing to arrive at all truth. She had access to few books, hence her acquirements in literary knowledge were very limited, up to the age of sixteen; but her enthusiastic love of all that was truly great and noble in weak humanity—of all that was sublime and beautiful in nature, clearly evinced that there was a volume of unwritten poetry in her soul.

At the age of sixteen she attended an academy located at O——, Ohio, taught by a lady who was a tolerably good scholar, but destitute of taste, as well as some other qualifications essential to a good teacher. Up to this period no line of jingling rhyme ever saw the light, but the usual routine of hard, dry studies, such as are said to expand and strengthen the mind, were taken up by her and pursued with the most unwavering perseverance; she being resolved not to be behind her class, notwithstanding all her previous disadvantages.

Examination day came at length, a day of much anxiety and disappointment to some, of triumph and success to others. Lurania had now found a medium through which she would pour out in one full gushing torrent all the enthusiasm of her mind. She read, or rather recited before a large audience, her "composition," which, notwithstanding the most positive interdiction of the teachers to the contrary, was received with the most gratifying applause. Envy and jealousy were now fairly set to work. It was a success which some illiberal and narrow minded spirits never forgave, especially as she possessed, at that time, a face and figure of more than common attraction.

Occasionally short pieces of poetry began to occupy the poet's corner in the country newspapers, over the signature of "LURANIA," while to improve her slender finances, she left the Academy and became a school teacher. By many Lurania was thought to be a genius, and truly has she paid the bitter penalty; for all that the most malicious detraction could fabricate, has been measured out to her, in such quality and quantity, that for a time she was quite overwhelmed with grief and despair. Her health gave way, and accompanied by some relatives she sought in the genial atmosphere of the South, that peace of mind and that restoration of health which she had so cruelly and unjustly lost. Upon her return all her former persecutions were again renewed; but still without any particular aim, she continued to warble forth her unpretending lays, like some lone bird, whose natural language is that of song.

With the most limited means she had no other resources but that of the ever-living fountains of her own heart, from whence to draw those beautiful images of all that is lovely, pure and good.

She eventually married Dr. W. B. Munday, a gentleman of fine feelings, and one who fully appreciated all her worth. Notwithstanding many vile aspersions he proved to be an indulgent husband, and a kind father, while those who knew him best, loved him most. He being a member of the Masonic fraternity, Mrs. Munday became acquainted with the principles of the "Mystic Brotherhood"—an order which claims to be founded upon Truth and Virtue, and whose leading star is Philanthrophy. The mission of Masonry struck with peculiar force her enthusiastic mind—hence the production of "ACACIAN LYRICS," a part of the present volume.

At the expiration of eight years, Dr. Munday died, leaving her with a broken constitution, and but illy calculated to struggle with the storms of life In her sad bereavement she returned to her father's house, and the family shortly after moved to the State of Illinois, where they are quietly pursuing the business of farming.

ACACIAN LYRICS.

JERUSALEM.

By the rivers of Babylon there we sat down; yea, we wept when we remembered Zion—*Bible.*

City of palms, of palaces and fountains,
Thou sit's a queen among thy sacred hills,
Begirt as by a tiara of mountains,
Thy ancient glory now my vision fills;
As oft the mind's swift rivers backward roll,
To glass thine image on their thousand rills;
Thou shrine of hope—the pilgrim's sacred goal,
Blest Mecca of the mind, and city of the soul.

Thy brazen gates, and consecrated fanes,
Thy many string'd and silvery sounding lyres,
Attuned alone to heaven's divinest strains,
Where erst the minstrel-king awoke the wires,
Until the soul seem'd fus'd in hallow'd fires,
Through time's dim vistas and its shadows gray,
Are brought to view as over dead empires,
Mouldering kingdoms, dust and pale decay,
Swift fancy's chariot speeds his thought-illumined way.

Pride of the earth, and chosen of God wert thou,
Enrobed in matchless strength and mystery,
A wondrous beauty crown'd thy peerless brow,
While joy and light divine abode with thee;
And when thy children in captivity
Were borne, they bowed in desolation,
And many a tearful glance was turned on thee,
While cries of woe, wailing and lamentation
In prayer went up by the dark streams of Babylon.

And now o'er Esdralon's palmy plain,
From Beitnumba's height I can behold,
Where Europe's hosts through blood and fiery rain,
With holy zeal in contests came of old;
Against the fierce Saladin's armies bold,
With trump and clarion strains and banners proud;
While swift the Paynim's arm'd chariot roll'd,
Through many a battle blast and red war-cloud,
Whose surges deep swept on in thunders long and loud.

And there with flying steed and glittering shield,
A Christian warrior clad in hauberk bright,
Sped onward o'er the dark ensanguin'd field,
Whose stalwart form absorb'd the startled sight;
Oh! know ye not that lion-hearted knight—
Great Plantagenet's brave and royal scion,—
Who came with mace of arms and sword to fight,
For Jesus and the cross and holy Zion,
Who was in peace a dove, in war an angry lion?

Where dwelt sweet peace among the cedarn shades,
E'er sound of trump was heard or battle glave,
My fancy turns, when Salem's beauteous maids,
In rippling Kedron's chaste and limpid wave,
Came down of old their snowy feet to lave ;
As night beams fall through groves of shadowy
    trees,
So softly bright the glance their dark eyes gave,
Their midnight tresses floating on the breeze,
Which oft in waving whispers came from Syrian seas.

Now I behold Gethsemene's fair bowers—
A light perfume floats through the mellow gloom,
Amidst whose dewy shades like soft snow show'rs,
Fall down the olive's wealth of virgin bloom ;
Where once to ransom us from certain doom,
Where shed those hallowed tears—those drops of
    woe,
A pledge of promised joy beyond the tomb,
Where Zion, free, shall dread no conquering foe,
And through supernal groves life's endless rivers flow.

And distant through the warm air shimmering,
Thy massive walls and towers of strength arise,
Bright spires and lofty turretts glimmering ;
While from the " Orient " robed in Tyrean dyes,
A queenly temple fills my wondering eyes,
Moriah's mystic fane, whose burnished dome,
Looms up as if to mock the bowing skies,

From many lands where Christian warriors come,
There tears and vows to blend above the holy tomb.

And now, high poised on fancy's soaring wings,
I fain would linger o'er the temple's shrine:
A heavenly radiance round about thee clings,
As mirror'd on my heart thy splendors shine—
Thy beauty wraps my soul, O! fane divine,
Where once of old in silken bonds, *three sons of
    light*,
With purpose high and mystic word and sign,
Together met, amid thy wonders bright,
That shone like flashing stars upon the brows of night

But now a change comes o'er my spirit's vision,
And Judah's pristine glories proudly bright—
So strangely fair they almost seem'd elysian—
Like rainbow dreams are sweeping out of sight;
Thy palm crown'd hills and vales are scorched with
    blight,
Thy marble fountains bound with burning chains;
A sable veil dark as the wings of night,
Hangs like a funeral pall above thy plains,
Thy ivy mantled walls and desecrated fanes.

No arch triumphal now is borne aloft;
No classic porticoes exclude the ray
Of Sol's hot radiance; no lute-notes soft,
Of Hebrew maid, as in the elder day

Blent with the wind's low voices float away,
Thy stately pageantries have vanish'd all—
A mournful glory wraps thee in decay,
While from the turkman's parapetted wall,
Is heard afar the "loud muezzin's solemn call."

Alas! for thee, my spirit inly weeps,
O, Jerusalem! a tearless sorrow reigns
In the far holy of my bosom's deeps;
My grieving lyre in solemn pean-strains
Awakes for thee, and mournfully complains.
Yet ever floating through my yearning dreams,
Bright glimpses come from heaven's celestial plains,
Where the redem'd shall quaff eternal streams,
And ransom'd Zion crown'd with light triumphant
    beams.

Masonic Song.

Sound the full chorus in anthems of praise,
To Him the Grand Master, the "ancient of days,"
Whose realm is all space, and whose temple the sky,
Whose portals are guarded by angels on high;
Where through the wide arching in beauty around,
Rise upheaving pillars of wisdom profound;

Begirt with his strength—in glory and might,
He reigns the great fountain of Spirit and Light.

Lo! an angel of love our bleak world has bless'd;
Be joyful each heart, for our heavenly guest
With purpose most holy and mission sublime,
Hath lived through the wrecks and the tempests of time—
Hath shed through the gloom of our passion-rent way,
Her soft tears of mercy like showers of May;
And deep is the light of her radient eyes,
As the beams of Hesperus in orient skies.

Like the sound of a flute to the slumberer's ear,
Or the music of harps from some hallow'd sphere,
Doth the tones of her voice in soft euphonies fall,
On the sorrowing heart through the desolate hall.
From the pale brow of pain the death-dews away,
She hath brush'd with her pinions, bright as the day:
While the sad orphan babes, to soothe and to bless,
She hath lull'd to sweet dreams in her gentle caress.

She hath a fair chaplet of emblems, entwin'd
With roses and lillies and cassias combined,
For the brows of our brethren, that fadeless shall bloom,
In the Lodge of the Spirit beyond the dark tomb;
Where the roses of love forever wax bright,
And the lilies of purity stainlessly white;

Where from evergreen bowers the "faithful" are
 crown'd,
And cassias immortal bloom ever around.

THE THREE FRIENDS AND THE JEWEL.

"The veil of the temple is rent, the builder is smitten, and we are raised from the tomb of transgression."

> At length, through time's expanded sphere,
> Fair science speeds her way;
> And warm'd by truth's refulgence clear,
> Reflects the kindred ray.
> A second fabric's towering height,
> Proclaims the sign restor'd;
> From whose foundation brought to light,
> Is drawn the mystic word.—*Masonic Ode.*

In Salem's palmy city dwelt,
 Far back in the olden time,
Three friends, who, round one alter knelt,
 Of mystic faith sublime.
A spirit net-work o'er them hung,
 Of fellowship and love;
And sweet their hearts according tones,
 As choral hymns above.

When soft beneath a crimson flood,

The lesser lights had set;
In silken bonds of brotherhood,
Those friends in silence met.
Within a secret chamber high,
Of Zion's hallow'd fane;
Where flashed along the guilded walls,
Bright rays like golden rain.

There, lock'd within a casket fair,
A priceless jewel lay,
Brighter than Neptune's burning gems,
Or morning's rosy ray.
And each possess'd the power to gaze,
Upon that jewel's light;
Serene and fair its lucid rays,
As starry eyes of night.

And thus the mystic brothers spoke,
As taught by lips divine;
Not one alone of us shall take,
The treasure from its shrine;
But met together, then, oh! then,
The casket's hidden store,
Shall bless our yearning sight again,
Its wonted radiance pour.

'Twas thus they parted—friend with friend,
With many a holy sign,

As low in solemn prayer they bent,
  Around the sacred shrine.
Time's heavy throb kept slowly on,
  And brought the trysting hours;
But one had pass'd the shad'wy vale,
  To rest in Eden bowers.

And in that consecrated place,
  They wistful gazed around;
Yet saw they not that one kind face,
  Through all the still profound.
Alas! the silver chord was loos'd,
  And seal'd the sacred lore;
While locked from sight the glowing gem,
  Must lie forever more!

Saids't thou forever more? Ah! no,
  For through our being's night,
The peerless gem doth softly shed,
  Its floods of spirit light,
And thus by hope and faith in Him,
  Who wept and died to save,
Our ransom'd souls will bask in light,
  And triumph o'er the grave.

Stanzas for the Year.

"Now I beseech you, brethren, by the name of our Lord Jesus Christ, that ye all speak the same thing, and that there be no divisions among you; but that ye all be perfectly joined together in the same mind, and in the same judgment."—*Cor.* 1 *Chap.* 10 *verse.*

"According to the grace of God which is given unto me, as a wise master builder, I have laid the foundation, and another buildeth thereon. But let every man take heed how he buildeth thereupon.—*Cor.* 3*d Chap.* 10 *verse.*

  Time! eldest born of elder day,
  The silent parent of decay;
 In the urn of the past, he has consigned,
 With the centuries old which he leaves behind,
   The year that's past away.
  Hail, all hail! the New Year's come,
  Strike the harp and sound the drum;
  Lo! we're hastening to the time,
  Of those greetings most sublime,
   In the great millenium.

  Awake! and work while yet 'tis day,*
  The night soon comes, make no delay;
  Earth's weeping ones—His precious poor,
  Have claims upon your love—your store,
   Go smooth their thorny way.
  "Brothers of the mystic tie,"

Hast thou heard the orphan's cry?—
To the sick hast given relief?
Hast thou stay'd the widow's grief?
    And check'd the mourner's sigh?

Say—what the work thy hands have sought,
Tell, what the joys thy deeds have brought?
O'er the old year's varied track,
Cast thy mental vision back—
    Hast in the quarry wrought?
Brother, of the social band,
O'er the sea in every land,
Tell us if in love thou hast,
Sought to shed those glories vast,
    Of Him the Master Grand?

Know'st thou of our faith sublime
We brethren have in every clime,
Who feel the same good shepherd's care—
Alike his love and beauty share
    Through all life's trial-time?
Then strive in harmony to dwell,
And every stormy passion quell,
Till through our Father's heavenly grace,
We reach that bless'd, most holy place
Where ceaseless anthems swell.
Though darkly now, in yon bright sky
We'll see each other eye to eye;

Our work of love and duty done,
And passed the " veils "—acceptance won,
In that Grand Lodge on High.

Lines

On the death of Austin W. Morris, Esq., who died at his residence in Indianapolis, June 20, 1851, and who was, at the time of his decease, and for some years previously, Grand Secretary of the Grand Masonic Lodge of the State of Indiana.

> Speak low the place is holy to the breath,
> Of awful harmonies, of whispered prayer;
> Tread lightly, for the sanctity of death,
> Broods with a voiceless influence on the air,
> Stern. yet serene, a reconciling spell,
> Each troubled billow of the soul to quell.
> *Mrs. Hemans.*

There's mourning in our mystic hall,
   For there's a vacant place—
A missing voice—a proud foot fall,
   And kind familiar face,
Far from our transient sphere away,
Hath pass'd to climes of endless day.

Silence and gloom are brooding round
   In fitful shadows pale;

And o'er our hearts a grief profound,
  Sits like a sable veil:
The eyes of light are dim with woe,
The voice of joy suppressed and low.

From out the firmament of thought,
  A spirit star hath fled ;
A column strong with beauty fraught;
  Hath fall'n among the dead ;
A sacred taper hath expir'd,
A weary soul to rest retir'd.

Thou art gone to dwell with angel bands,
  The happy and forgiv'n,
In thy father's house not made with hands,
  Eternal in the heaven,
Where grief and pain shall enter not,
And earthly emblems are forgot.

O ! yes ! we know thou'st found the shore,
  Of still and quiet streams :
Of pastures green, where ever more,
  Thou'lt bask in glory's beams :
That " bourne " for which the sad soul yearns,
From whence no traveler returns.

Thou't laid aside the trestle board,
  The compasses and square ;
Thou hast resign'd the purple robe,

For brighter raiments there—
The toil is o'er, the work is done,
The capstone laid, the triumph won.

Thou'st passed within the inner veil,
   In that bless'd lodge above;
And thee will angel wardens hail,
   In fellowship and love;
Where many a harp's seraphic tone,
Shall sound around the great "white throne."

The mem'ry of thy deeds of love,
   Are lingering with us yet,
Like incense floating from above—
   Those tones shall we forget?
Ah! no, by all that's felt below,
The orphan's grief, the widow's woe.

And kindly round our brotherhood,
   A silken chain thou'st flung;
'Twas sweet as heaven's dewy flood,
   That on the mountains hung;
And mercy, love and friendship there
Were woven in the linklets fair.

'Twas thine the wounded heart to heal,
   The tempest passions quell;
'Twas thine for human ills to feel,

ACACIAN LYRICS.

Where earth-born sorrows dwell;
And each descenting heart and mind,
In gentle fellowship to bind.

Thine ark is safely wafted o'er
    The surging waves of time;
There thou shalt quaff unceasing lore,
    From streams and founts sublime;
Rivers of joy there flow along,
Like one unceasing tide of song.

Brother, within thy lethean tomb,
    An evergreen we fling;
As fadeless shall thy spirit bloom
    In one perennial spring;
Then rest thee on, until thy dust again,
The last trump wake—" so mote it be"—amen.

―――

To a Friend

Of aught there is that's sweet,
In the rude tones that from my lute-strings ring;
    Sweet friend, wilt thou not kindly greet,
        This offering.

Could I but pour a strain

The trembling strings in cypress gloom which long
Hath hung, I'd sweep, if thou but deign,
    To hear my song.

When but an artless child,
Of glorious fame I had a glowing dream;
Around my brain the fancy wild,
    Is still my theme.

And do ambition's fires,
Thou't ask—burn in fond woman's gentle soul?
And doth it wake those deep desires,
    Beyond control?

Say, what to thee is fame,
Again thou'lt ask—although thro' storm and shade,
In life's dark day thou win'st a name,
    That may not fade?

It is to be enshrined,
Within the hearts of those—the gifted few—
With noble and exalted minds,—
    The good and true?

I'd teach my brother man,
To love the pure—the poor and weak defend
To be the orphan's guardian,—
    The widow's friend

Breathe words of solace where
The heart is broke, and burns the throbbing brain,

And soothe the soul o'er which despair,
    A sovereign reigns.

A lovely wreath I'd fling
Round stern celestial virtue's chastened brow,
Unto her shrine sweet offering bring—
    Before it bow.

Thus I would write my name,
In flame upon the arches of the sky,
And o'er my harp would fling a wreath of fame
    That should not die.

An Allegory

Roaring adversity's relentless winds,
Swept madly o'er the world's dark wilderness;
When through its trackless wastes and drear confines,
All sad and pale with want and weariness,
Wandered a lone and mournful orphan child.
  A patient grief sat on her features mild,
While worn and thin around her fragile form,
As if to shield her from life's fearful storm,
Its last scant gift pale poverty had flung,
Which now in tattered shreds and ruined fragments
    hung.

Beside the rough and thorn-encompass'd way
Sin's horrid imps were howling seen to stray;
Gaunt Famine turned to heaven its leader eyes,
And rent the troubled air with shrieking cries;
Despair with livid lips, and frenzied laugh,
An opiate cup of lethean wine did quaff,
While deeply dyed in darkness, flame and blood,
Stalked grimly near Crime's hydra-headed brood.

In this bleak world, ah! whither should she fly?
No friends, no home, oh! could she choose but die;
But hark! as from the skies, with silvery tone,
A voice was heard to say "let her alone."
  From the uncertain sin-beclouded way,
Her weak unguarded feet to lead astray,
An ignus fatuous light gleam'd from afar,
As shines upon the night some isolated star.
And from soft Pleasure's elfin guarded isle,
The murm'ring winds a wild'ring incense flung;
While on the sea-washed rocks with Circean wile,
Temptation's soul-alluring syrens sung;
Where many a subtle coil of woe they weave,
The earth-sick, way-worn pilgrim to deceive.
How dark the vale of woe that lay beyond—
How fathomless the gulf that blacken'd yawn'd;
She heeded not the Stygean surges roar,
And, as if some spirit-strain once more
To hear, the child her ravished ear bent low,
And from her violet eyes wip'd off the dews of woe.

'Twas not Temptation's mad'ning strains she heard,
But sweeter far, a charm'd and mystic word;
And with that sound which she knew passing well,
Was linked a sign of talismanic spell;
Dispersing every earth-born grief and fear,
And bound with magic power the child's enraptured ear.

   Gliding upon the gloom,
A sweet voice rippled musical and clear,
Inspired as the rapt wisdom of a sear,
Yet as a mother's, soft, when from its troubled sleep,
Her darling frightened wakes to sob and weep,
She lulls again with gentle songs to rest,
The sobbing one upon her faithful breast.

Lo! on time's changing ocean dark and vast,
A heaven-directed barque was launched at last;
An angel guide with loving eyes of light,
Controll'd it through the foggy veils of night;
Faith watched the helm with heavenward look serene
While Charity, sweet maid, with tender mein,
Stood near, and smiling Hope with rosy wings,
From joy's enchanted lyre of golden strings,
Sweet strains awoke, to cheer the drooping child.
Across the wildering waste of waters wild.
Laced by a golden strand was seen to smile,
Far off, a gem-like palm-embower'd isle;
Where cloudless arched the soft cerulean skies,
And light aromas floated sweet as summer sighs;
Where Harmony, that blest and gentle river,

Its chiming songs went murmuring;
Soft as the breath that thro' the palm leaves quiver
Or the light waving of an angel's wing.
Amid the incense-breathing bloom a strain
Of joy in floating melodies arose,
Where truth-illumined shone a skiey fane,
Whose time-defying walls stood forth in calm repose,
Wisdom and strength adorned in columned pride,
While beauty's graceful arch bent o'er the portals wide.
And there the orphan's rosy childhood hours,
Went by, list'ning among the joy-born flowers
To life's great lyre, whose chaunting tones profound,
Arose in many an under-swell and spirit sound.
Wave after wave of time went swelling on—
In sinless dreams her childhood hours were gone,
And still the guide stood near and gently spake,
As breezy murmurs over still woods break.

"Fair child, doth not thy spirit sometimes yearn
For home beyond, where ageless planets burn?
Those orbs, when floating thro' the blue sublime,
That sung of old creation's glorious hymn;
A world of light dost thou not sometimes deem,
Floats viewless o'er immensity's broad stream,
Where mortal ear ne'er heard its raptures full,
Nor eye had seen its treasures beautiful?"

The orphan sighed—"Ah! why should soul of mine,
For joys more pure or visions more divine,

E'er seek beyond the sky-bound spheres to roam?
Am I not bless'd and free in this terrestial home?"
The angel smiled—" Ah! poor weak child of clay,
Know'st thou ye are but insects of a day?
To-morrow these pale children of decay,
Smote by the stygian breath shall pass away.
When on thy sight life's transient glories fade,
And strong upon thy heart death's fingers cold are laid,
  When all the sounds of life wax dim,
  And voices soft of seraphim,
  Upon thy faint ear call away,
  Wilt thou then pause to go.   Oh! say."
"Ah! no; if that I knew a world more fair,
Where enter not, nor pain—nor death—nor care."
"Then with thy spirit's proud bright eyes behold
That which the seers inspired song of old."
The orphan smiled and to the shore advanced,
As through a prison bright its spirit vision glanced.
And then the angel smiled with look benign,
"What seest thou fair child—sweet orphan mine?"
"An angel-peopled world—a brighter clime than this;
A land of more substantial joy—more radient bliss—
A Lodge of spirit light beyond the tomb,
Where beauteous bowers of deathless cassia bloom."
" 'Tis well—know'st thou a brother from yon lodge of
    light,
Came down in days of old to dwell?
Our King and great high Priest, whose wisdom bright,
Outshone the quenchless spheres.—Did he not tell,

Our brethren at the temple's shrine,
Who heard with sacred awe his words divine?
'Behold! ye have a mission to fulfill,
Go ye, and do our Great Grand Master's will.'
So thou should'st likwise go, and like the ray
Of evening's sundown glories round thy way,
Let winged love, and star-eyed hope, and truth,
O'er all thy works prevail—go consecrate thy youth,
By deeds of holy faith and love divine,
In its aromal innocence to heaven's hallow'd shrine;
For time is but a brief ephemeral day,
Born like the flowers, to bloom and fade away.
But as for me, a more enduring toil is mine,
For have not I beheld vast kingdoms fall,
With all that's best, and bright, that's noblest or divine?
Upon my feet their ashes lie, while over all
The swift winged centuries sweep by
As mists of morning 'fore the sunlight fly;
And scattered round the wrecks of pale decay,
On many a surge of time are born away.
   Go, then, sweet orphan mine—bright heritor of heaven,
And when thy mission's done, thy clay-born sins forgiv'n,
Our souls again shall meet, rejoice, unite
In yon bright Lodge, amid the sons of light,
And may the word and sign as taught when time began,
Upon the lips of faith and hope, forever with thee dwell,

And shield thy heart from blight till heav'n-home be
   won,
And death and danger pass'd.   Sweet child, farewell."
The orphan waved a sign of hope and joy profound,
While sweet the angel smiled, and strewed his palm
   leaves round.

MISCELLANEOUS POEMS.

REMINISCENCES.

Respectfully inscribed to a graduate of Miami University.

" How warmly and vividly they rise,
    Those memories of the past ;
The flashing eye, the kindling cheek,
    As when I saw them last."

" Thy heart amid vulgar joys will aspire to something holier ; thine ambition, amid coarse excitements to something beyond thy reach. But deem not that this of itself will suffice for glory. It is but an imperfect and new born energy, which will not suffer thee to repose. As thou directest it, must thou deem it to be the emanations of thy evil genius or thy good.—*Sir E. L. Bulwer.*

Thou, of the lofty brow ! where proudly sits
Bright intellect enthron'd—where glowing thought,
Oft breaks its deep repose, thine azure eyes illume.
Oh ! could'st thou lend a kind indulgent ear,
For thee I'd sing in numbers wildly breath'd,
For thee I'd string my rustic harp anew,
If but the slumbering tones of memory's lyre
I could awake ; and from the misty past,
Old scenes, old faces, pleasant thoughts recall,
Back to thy mind like long forgotten strains
Of melody, which sometimes break upon the ear.

And thou hast wander'd—Where ? Hast seen the West?

In all its gorgeousness and solemn pride,
The prairie vast in lonely beauty dress'd,
From whose utmost verge,'twould seem the king of day,
Through the blue deeps his car of fire upwheels,
'Till past the viewless plains and rolling spheres,
Down-flashing far, his waning glow goes out
In seas of golden light, where warm and low,
The occidental skies in love bend down,
Like rainbow draperies o'er his evening couch.

And there amid the voiceless solitudes,
Thou hast beheld those vast and lonely tombs,
So strangely beautiful, where fall'n warriors sleep,
Upon whose brain-bewildering mysteries
The mildew page of time can shed no light;
And from sweet beds of nameless flowers didst hear
The low and melancholy winds arise,
And wildly sweep above the unknown dead,
In requiems sad their dirge-like melodies.
Hast thou a heart? I know, I feel, thou hast;
And, in her silent language, nature breathed
Her inspirations beautiful into its large recess;
Amid the solemn stillness round didst hear
It throb?—as if Divinity was stirr'd
Within thy soul's profound; didst kneel, didst bend
In adoration on the soft green turf?
As if within the area of some cathedral vast,
While poetry in measured numbers leap'd
From off thy lips, as touched by sacred fire?

Art thou a poet? Aye! it must be so.
Thine eyes have not been blind, nor deaf thine ears,
Or from the external world have ever failed
To the internal world of mind to make
A due report. The heaven-descended maid
Her radient impress on thy lofty brow
Hath left, while soft the shadows of the mind,
Like vapory clouds, lift soft and airily away;
And all created things, with stupid gaze
Regarded by the dull and prosing mind,
To thee half spiritualized appear,
And in prismatic glories seem to shine.

Oh! who would leave the pure and bright creations
Of the world of thought for dull and cold reality?
Who would not ever revel 'midst his own
Imaginings—although his helicon
Should sometimes prove like mine, a bitter fount
Of tears! Hast ever felt thy mind oppress'd
With thrilling, keen conceptions of the grand,
Sublime and beautiful? Doth thy heart yearn
For truth and purity more infinite?
Thy soul imbuing with a lofty sense
Of its high nature and majestic destiny,
While far above the earth—its carking cares
And sordid fripperies—it seems to soar?
If thus thy mind is delicately organized,
Susceptibilities possessing keen,
Amidst this harsh and jarring world thou mayst

Not mingle, or dwell among distorted things,
Cold and unlovely to the soul and sense;
Some rude and reckless hand will break
The music of thy soul—disturb its harmony
Come! let us wander—rememb'rst my face?
I essayed to say—along fair Tempe's vales
And drink Parnassian dews.

     The roseat hues
Of youth are blooming still in richness on thy cheek:
Perchance life's summer may not close,
E'er thou mayst write within the portals wide,
Of Pindu's hoary fane—upon its lofty walls
A Poet Laureat's immortal name.

   Where am I? I left thee journeying on,
Amid the sky-bound prairie's lonely solitudes,
Striving to gain some island home, before the fall
Of eventide, and when its dim and woody ailes
At length didst reach, and safely hous'd thyself
Within some rustic's shelter rude—what thoughts
Of painful sweetness then thy lonely mind employ'd;
And home—" sweet home "—friends and companions
  dear,
Arose as with a spell mysterious,
And pass'd in sweet review within thy memory.
Friend! an aching pang—a mystic chord,
Is 'twin'd around that little treasur'd word;
And each remove from a dear cherish'd one,

As 'twere by tension adds a keener pang.
Thou hast return'd—thy roving feet once more,
Have sought the spacious halls and sylvan shades,
Of proud Miami, famed for classic lore.
The boon companions of thy youth again thou'lt meet.
And press the eager hand of friendship warm,
And in old faces read new welcomes home.

Thou'lt tread those social classic halls once more,
Where new fledged politicians oft essay'd
To soar, on fancy's wings bombastically sublime;
And again thou'lt wander through the twilight groves
Of that old temple, as in boyhood's days,
And hear their wind-waked melodies arise,
And float through all their dark and dim arcades,
Till cradled in the tall and whispering grass,
They're hushed to rest.

'Tis a sweet spot, and like
A paradise, but that no dark-eyed houri's hymn
Is ever heard along the sounding aisles.
Dost recollect those golden hours of bliss
Long passed—When oft with book in hand thou did'st
Beneath those sylvan shades recline, where oft
The antique woods in vernal beauty rang,
With first attempts of youthful eloquence,
As even of old the thunderer the forum shook?

How oft the echoes woke in answering strains,
To Homer's classic songs—the story sad,

Of proud and hapless Illium's fall,
Those records old of war-like deeds and god-like men.
  And here thou'st listen'd to the empassion'd strains
Of Byron's deep toned melancholy lyre,
Wondering in strange bewilderment if he could be,
Or man, or fiend, or of celestial birth,
As oft with mad'ning sweep he rent its quivering strings.
  And o'er immortal Shakespear's wizzard songs,
In rapturous admiration thou hast bent :
While sweet Ophelia's woes, and Desdemona's wrongs,
And Juliet's touching love, and hump-back'd Richard's crimes.
Of the enchanter's power gave ample proof,
And of his searchings deep within the still
And viewless workings of the human heart.
  But now my simple reedy song is done,
For well I know that thou art wearied grown,
With my untutor'd lays and harpings rude.
In its accustomed nook my rustic lyre
I'll hang—but yet perchance in shady covert hid,
Thou'lt hear me warble forth again my wood notes wild.
Till then, farewell !

The "Lone Tree," and the Solitary Grave.

To Oscar.

There many a bird of weary wing,
  Like Noah's wandering dove may rest;
Its grateful shades a joyance bring
  Unto the wayworn trav'ler's breast.

Bear high thy proud majestic boughs thou tree,
  And wide thy kind protecting branches spread;
For there is one at rest, who sleeps by thee,
  Bold and serene—our cherished, changeless dead!

How oft my dreaming thoughts go back
  Thro' the misty vale of sighs and tears;
To bask along the flow'ry track,
  In the light of my childhood's years.
Its sense of joy, how deep and full,
  How wild and high its burning dreams;
Life's visions shone all beautiful,
  As through a prism nature gleams.

Oh! then the fondest hopes were mine,
  With patient zeal my mind could soar
To distant joys I deemed divine,
  Which now my heart can feel no more.
And as I muse, I'm thinking now
  Of one asleep we loved so well,
With placid mien and thoughtful brow,
  Who by our hearthstone used to dwell.

And through the might of kindred ties,

Her angel presen'' now draws near;
While with my spirit's yearning eyes,
I can behold the loved one dear.
How spirit-like her azure eyes,
  How soft her voice and bland her smile;
E'en as the light of summer skies,
  That glows above some ocean isle.

How mild and sweet her gentle ways,
  How pure the fountains of her mind,
Which often gushed in saphic lays,
  Like plaintive harp-strains of the wind.
Bathed in Pierien founts, her soul
  Wore the bright hues of musing thought;
Dreaming of some enchanted goal,
  As if from heaven those hues were caught.

Ah! sweet as Polyhymenia's song,
  The mournful music of her lyre,
In classic numbers flowed along,
  As oft she swept each trembling wire.
No more, alas! that spirit lute,
  With trembling lays our hearts shall thrill;
The tender voice we loved is mute,
  And the throbbing pulse is still.

There waves a solitary tree,
  Upon the prairie's distant verge;
And pining winds are mournfully
  Awaking many a solemn dirge;

And where the dreaming star-eyed flowers,
　　Their voiceless hymns of joy around,
Are singing to the summer hours,
　　Her place of solemn rest is found.

And oh! 'tis consecrated ground,
　　For there she sleeps alone—alone—
While viewless spirits hov'ring round,
　　Methinks have claimed it for their own.

Song of the Genii.

"There is a principle of the soul superior to all external nature; and through that principle we are capable of surpassing the orders and systems of the world, and participating the immortal life, and the energy of the sublime celestials.
　　*　　*　　*　　When the soul is elevated to natures above itself, it deserts the orders to which it is awhile compelled, and by a religious magnetism is attracted to another and loftier with which it blends and mingles.—*Zanoni, or the Secret Order.*

When the earth is slumber-bound,
In the shades of night profound,
As the gush of silver streams,
All the starry host of beams
Shed their dewy glories round;
When the chill is on the ground
And nor step, nor voice, nor sound

Breaks the solemn stillness round;
And the moon of ashy hue,
Sails along the deeps of blue,
In her barque of dreamy light,
With her sails of cloudlets white,
And her figure-head in sight,
Through all the jewel'd hours of night,
O'er the land and o'er the sea,
Mortal, we are there with thee.
In the silence dark and deep,
When the weary are asleep,
While nor cloud, nor speck, nor stain,
Marks the cold etherial plain;
Then to us a charm is given,
Not of earth, but fraught of heaven.
Then we kindly vigils keep,
And the willing senses steep,
In our changing tears and smiles,
And the slumb'rer's thoughts beguile,
In the rosy land of dreams,
Of spirit-lyres and singing streams,
  Fancy-wrought
  Wing'd with thought, far away.

In the shadow of the woods,
Where the roar of falling floods,
Breaks in echoes o'er the hill,
By the lakelet dark and still,
In the golden sunset's glow,

In the vallies warm and low
Mid the rainbow-tinted flow'rs,
Through the sylvan walls and bowers,
In the homes of mirth or woe,
Where e'er the wand'ring zephyrs go
In the light and in the shade,
With the soul of any grade,
Wrought of heaven, or earth, or air,
We are here, and we are there,
We are with thee every where.
And around thee ever dwell,
Like the spirit of a spell,
Or the essence of a dream,
Or the life of perish'd streams
Like the shade of banished sound,
Or the pulse of night profound
Or the music of the dews,
Never known, never seen,
These are spirit-like I ween.

When the meteor mild and high,
Flashes down the midnight sky,
And its lone sepulchral gleam,
Glows within the lambent stream,
Swift its birth and pale its beam,
As the mem'ry of a dream;
And the glow-worm through the gloom,
Lights his small ephemeral fires

Where the ivy wreathes the tomb,
And the tones of orphean wires,
Tremble in the tall rank grass,
While through the steep and rocky pass,
Shrieks the owlet's doleful song,
Waking echoes dull and long;
Where nor bloom, nor verdure smil'd,
Midst the herdless rocklets wild;
Up the glen and o'er the marsh,
Where the sounds are dull and harsh—
We'll be with thee then and there,
Tho' thou seek'st to wander where,
Aught of spirit good or ill,
Ne'er shall follow against thy will.
  Mortal, if thou seek'st relief,
From a soul-o'er-mastering grief,
Or from doubt, or dread, or fright,
Or with step and bosom light,
Wand'rest with the joyous throng,
Where rich harpings peal along;
What e'er thy wishes, hopes or quests,
What, tho' we seem unbidden guests,
What e'er betide thee, good or ill,
The voiceless Genii guides thee still.

Osceola's Lament.

Here in these lonely prison walls,
    Seminola's chief is laid;
The white man from his forest halls,
    Has lur'd him and betray'd.

Here in the white man's prison chain'd,
    Like an eagle caged I pine;
The free blood coursing through my veins,
    My spirit unresigned.

No more I'll bound along the vale,
    With a kindred warrior band;
No more my steed will snuff the gale,
    When foes invade our land.

The war-knife we'll no more unsheath,
    To wreak our vengeance fell;
Or hear the loud, clear, war-whoop shrill,
    Or the forest-brave's wild yell.

Our council fires no longer gleam,
    Their ashes now are cold;
And far from Pensacola's stream,
    Wander our warriors bold.

No more we'll launch the bark canoe
    From off the pebbly shore;
The finny tribe no more pursue,
    With swiftly dashing oar.

MISCELLANEOUS PIECES.   43

No more the pipe its fragrant fumes,
   Sends curling round our heads :
Dead silence wraps in sullen gloom
   The spot where braves have bled.

No more around the watch-fire's blaze,
   Will forest maidens dance ;
Or Osceola e'er embrace,
   Or meet the " White Fawn's" glance.

The pliant bow lies all unbent,
   The arrrow now is broke :
The red man's pride and power is wrent,
   His neck must wear the yoke.

Great Spirit ! are the red man's wrongs,
   As nothing in thy sight ?
Is treachery and crooked tongues,
   Approved by thee as right ?——

But hark ! the pale face may be near,
   Exulting o'er the red man's pain.
No sigh from Osceola shall he hear,
   He may not hear a Chief complain.

When storms arise and round us sweep,
   The bending willow quakes ;
But proudly stands the stately oak
   It scorns to bend—and, breaks.

A smile of sullen scorn his lip now wreath'd,
   It quivered—trembled—'twas the last ;

Proud Osceola now no longer breathed—
His spirit dark and grim had pass'd!

Musings,

On the Death of a Class-mate.

Look yet on this pale face,
Dim grows the semblance on man's heart impress'd,
Come near and bear the beautiful to rest.

Spring shall return,
Bringing the earth her lovely things again,
All—save the loveliest far—a voice—a smile—
A young sweet spirit gone.—*Mrs. Hemans.*

Alas! that flow'ers should loose their blushing hues,
That fairest ones are ever earliest to depart,
That autumn with its chilling breath should come
To kill and scatter round the verdant leaf;
That time should smite the open brow of youth,
And leave his wrinkled impress there; that its glad voice
Should e'er be hush'd—and o'er the red ripe lips,
And radient eyes, that death should set his seal.
She whom I sing was fair; e'en as the brow
Of night's pale regent, whose enchanted beams,
Stole down the Latmian hills of old and charm'd
Endymeon's heart to joy, and Paphean dreams.

Aye! fair—and there were those perchance, who
    deemed
Her beautiful; but there was that within,
Her spirit's temple, that woke a charm more potent
Than sweet beauty's self can fling upon the past.
A soul, pure, of child-like innocence and fraught
With the celestial fires of angel poesy.
She had early learn'd the joy of nature's
Worship; for unto her all things assumed
Prismatic hues—a deeper charm did wear,
Than unto minds of common mold. The fields
And plains in sunny beauties dress'd; the wood's
Dark solitudes—the shad'wy lake within
Whose breast serene, in silence floats each form
Of nature's charms—the pulseless spheres of night,
Like ageless sentinels, that keep their watches cold
Along the silent sky's far infinite,—
The stately moon in her cold beauty dress'd,
The brilliant sunset—gold tinged and crimson dy'd,—
The fitful music of æolean winds,
As they would rise and sweep the ocean's crest,
And through the dim woods wake their murmurs deep;
The silvery chime of many mingling streams,
And the blithe songs of summer birds; these,
With all their varied charms, sank deep within her
    heart,
And stir'd the placid waters of her soul,
Which gushing, flow'd away in streams
Of sweetest melody.

And she had musings,
Strange, yet sacred; musings, such as may dwell
Within the breast of innocence alone:
For oft would she in dreamy reveries 'rapt,
Recline upon the soft green sward and watch
The towering clouds as they would rise and float,
Like panoramic scenes in mountain strength
And majesty away.

And upward still,
Her thoughtful gaze was fixed, as if to pierce
The far beyond—and with intelligence
Divine, to hold converse—while the mute joy
Of her pure soul bedew'd her eyes' soft azure,
As though sh'd caught a tissuey dream of heaven!
And oft her parian hand amid the lute strings
Wander'd for strains inspired—and when they came,
The charm'd soul trembled—thrill'd, and was absorbed
In music; now sweet and low, then wild and high,
As the strange gush of Memnon's fabled sounds,
Whose surges deep stole round the column'd arches
Of the antique fane, and in the fret-work,
Of the lofty dome, and down the time worn walls
The mystic voice expired.

E'en now my heart
Thrills with a sense most sad of melancholy joy,
As recollection stalks along the past,
When gently link'd in friendship's rose-wreathed chain,

I've wandered oft along the twilight aisles
Of some far echoing wood, with her who oft
In dalliance fond would smooth my sadden'd brow,
And round her playful finger 'twin'd my careless hair.
But she, amid the mournful cadences
Of sounds autumnal; of falling leaves,
And faded flowers, hath lately gone to rest.
O! would I might recall those hours serene,
And backward roll the lethean waves of time,
And from oblivion's ebon vortex glean
The treasures of the past.

    Alas! no more
Shall her bland voice, or sunny smile, or words
So full of trustful hope e'er fall again
Upon my riven heart, or shine above
My lonely way; for with those halcyon hours
My brightest dreams of hope and joy were blent,
Now, each succeeding one that onward rolls,
Bears ample record of my falling tears.
Lo! where yon willow with the cypress vine,
In grief-like silence twines its fibrous limbs,
A hillock rises green, and the low winds,
In fitful gusts, wail through the tall grass mournfully,
A death-dirge o'er the tomb; the lost of earth;—
'Tis there she lies, in awful, sweet repose.
Spring, with her bland and gentle breath shall kiss
The earth again, upon whose glowing breast,
In radient bloom shall smile the sta eyed flowers,

And the extinguish'd flame may be relit,
But spring no more shall e'er the rosy hues
Of life to the still features of the voiceless dead
Restore, or e'er the spirit-fires relume.
And yet I would not summon back the soul
Departed—fetterless, pure, and free—or wake
It to life's miseries. I would not compass
That celestial spark within a woe-worn tenement
Of sickly clay, though cold and damp her narrow bed
And her repose be long and dreamless,
Although no orient beam of morning sun,
Or evening moon, or melancholy stars,
Shall gleam along the dim sepulchral halls,
To gild their darkness, or music-murmurs
Of charming streams, or songs of birds or wind,
The long monotonous night may ever break.
Ah! no—I would not now unlock eternity,
Or e'er disturb the death-bound slumberer's rest.
Yet, careless wand'rer, step not rudely o'er
The sacred dust, lest ye shall crush
The violets there that blossom on her breast.
They hang their timid heads and weep all night,
Until the morning sun with genial ray,
Shall kiss the trembling tears away.
The modest weepers crush not, for a semblance fair,
We've found in them of her who sleeps below.
Like pleasant thoughts, or evanescent hues
Which curtain sunset with their gorgeous dyes;
Like a soft dream, or dying melody

That leaves no trace behind—so her mild spirit
Took its flight, and the soul-lit radiance
Of her deep-blue eyes went out forever!

ROSSEAU'S HELOISE.
Adjuration.

Can'st thou forget, that solemn day
When warm in youth I gave the world away?
Can'st thou forget what tears that moment fell,
When lost to thee, I bade the world farewell?—*Pope.*

Deep are thy fountains love, thy spells how strong,
Thy draughts are poisonous, and thy joy thrills pain;
Yet is there bliss in your refin'd excess, tho' long
The sad o'er burthen'd soul may strive in vain,
To rend from off the mind the burning chain,
In wild idolatry that mad'ning binds,
Unsought the throbbing heart, and o'er wrought brain;
Ah! sacred, pure and bless'd, is love that finds,
One heart alone—one soul—one sacred shrine.

And I have lov'd e'en thus, until my brain,
Went wild, and in my spirit's wretchedness,
Have curs'd me for that worship. All in vain
Have striven the spell to break. Oh! who could guess
That those sweet dreams would bring such deep distress?

Ah! ne'er again such love my breast shall know,
For it became a madness, and did press
The life-blood from my heart, like lava streams to flow
O'er my scorch'd eye-balls, burning with their woe.

Years have roll'd on, and o'er my cheek and brow,
Pale sorrow's impress ever sits to tell,
That all the past is but a waste, as now,
A fearful, pleasing dream, on which I dwell,
With such strange happiness, striving to quell
These passion-hopes. Hear me ye gods! I bow
In tearless anguish which my bosom swells,
And 'fore the shrine of heaven this last wild vow
I'll breathe: love to nought earthly shall my lips avow

Hear me, ye burning spheres! behold it, heaven!
Thou melancholy moon and glorious sun;
Bear ye all witness, how my heart was given
With its proud hopes and quenchless love to one
Who sighs with blighted heart o'er joy-dreams done,
And far from me by cruel fate--alone--
Was o'er the waste of disappointment driven;—
Love wept as oft it mark'd the wreck begun,
O'er the free hearts it scarcely just had won.

Alas! for me the wreck'd-crush'd, and heart riv'n,
There smiles no future dream of hope or rest.
Ah! why to me was life so joyless given?
Which seems a fearful and mysterious jest;
Yet shall the earth-worn pilgrim still be bless'd,

If in the unrefunding tomb there is repose,
For soon within its halls I'll be a guest,
Heedless alike of all life's follies and its woes,
Where love forgets its tears, and hate its foes.

Autumn Winds are Sighing.

A Dirge.

"Why do ye rustle on your dark wings, ye whistling storms of the sky?"—Ossian.

Sad autumn winds are sighing,
Sweet summer gems are dying,
The forest leaves are lying,
    All withered, scorch'd and sear.

And through the air are flying,
Strange birds that fast seem hieing,
To a land with ours vieing,
    E'er the yelling blasts were here.

The wind-god's wildly sweeping,
His lyre that erst was sleeping,
Midst modest violets weeping,
    Their sweet cerulean dew.

No silver founts are leaping,
The wood-nymphs fair are weeping,
And summer days are creeping,
    On to their sad adieu.

"The melancholy days are here,"
With mournful sounds and storm clouds drear,
Telling with many an emblem sear,
    We all shall pass away.

The blast is round me pealing,
A gloom o'er earth revealing;
O'er nature's cheek is stealing,
    The hectic of decay.

No choristers are singing,
No buds or flow'rets springing,
For battling sounds are ringing
    With the storm-trump's blast.

The circean song from pleasure's bower,
And leaf, and bird, and bud, and flower,
And springing fount, and summer hour,
    Are buried with the past.

Hollow winds are roaring,
Chill autumn rains are pouring,
All nature seems deploring,
    Her glowing beauties fled.

Moan! moan! ye sobbing winds,
Since in your wail, the sorrowing mind,
Of its wild griefs a semblance finds,
    Like us, ye wail the dead.

TO A YOUNG POETESS.

"Come let us wander,   *   *   *   *
I essay'd to say, along fair Tempe's vales,
And drink Parnassian dews."

Listen, oh, list! sweet minstrel maid,
    Upon whose thoughtful brow,
Parnassian wreaths are blooming laid,
    Bright songstress, hear me now.

Thou hast arous'd my slumbering lyre,
    Its "wood-notes" woke again;
While every thrilling spirit-wire,
    Yields back an answering strain.

I ween that thou art young and fair,
    Of mild and gentle ways;
With sad sweet eyes, and sunny hair,
    So tender are thy lays.

The plume tips of its viewless wings,
    Some fairy sprite doth sweep
Across thy lyre's electric strings,
    So full its tones and deep.

Thy song is like the winds that float,
    Among the autumn leaves;
Or like the ring-dove's plaintive note,
    So mournfully it grieves.

Where thou the early flow'rs did'st cull,

That grace thy mountain streams,
Did'st learn those musings beautiful—
Pure thoughts and holy dreams?

Ah! where the lofty "elm woods" rise,
The pine encircled hills,
That seem to emulate the skies,
Where gush thine own wild rills.

There hast thou learn'd that mystic lore,
While o'er thy musing mind,
A pensive joy sits evermore,
A happiness refined.

Say, gentle priestess of the lyre,
Amid thy heart's wild springs;
Hath felt unquenched no deep desire—
A hope that upward springs?

For joys more infinite and high,
For glories more sublime,
In yon pure world beyond the sky,
That soul-illumin'd clime?

And doth not through thy slumbers glide,
Some soft entrancing spell;
As though still watching by thy side,
Kind sister spirits dwell.

From angel Kathleen's dreamy eyes,
Didst inspiration quaff?

While on the evening wind's low sigh,
Was borne her syrean laugh.

For oh! may not the lost return?
　From their far realm of light—
The lov'd for whom our tried hearts yearn,
　Tell thou of visions bright!

I may not now behold thy face,
　In this our narrow sphere;
But in that blest and happy place,
　With those we cherished here;

With choral hymns may we not meet,
　Amid an angel throng;
Where we that seraph band shall greet,
　The sisterhood of song.

But hark! the pulse of time throbs on,
　And hush'd the answering strain,
The willow's sighing boughs upon,
　I'll hang my lyre again.

The Shipwreck.

*The queenly ship! brave hearts had striven,
And true ones died with her.*

I stood on the sea-wash'd beach alone,
Listening the ocean's solemn moan;
The winds were pillow'd on the waves,
Up-sparkling from their pearl-spar'd caves;
And swift the dolphin leap'd in light,
Like a radient meteor beaming bright,
Scathing the face of the glassy plain,
As it rose in air, then swam again.
All hush'd and calm was the deep serene,
When the shadowy form of a ship was seen,
Slow sailing onward to the land,
Of those who sought a kindred band.
Tell us ye winds—oh! did not they,
Of friends and homes far, far away,
Bright dreams of hope and joy create?
Or dream'd they of the coming fate,
That o'er their visions fair should cast,
Its shadows dark to kill and blast
Each hope-born dream? Oh! fearful night,
When loved ones there with eyes of light,
Still sought the shore with yearning sight,
Who thought of some sweet happy day,
Ere childhood's hours had pass'd away,
Spent in some consecrated bower:
Or parting words, or joyous hour.

Or low sweet voice, or murmur'd vow,
Or smile of one that's sleeping now.
Alas! alas—no more—no more—
Those lov'd ones e'er shall press the shore,
For lo! a cloud in the sun-set sky,
Caught the quick glance of the seaman's eye,
And long on its darkness in dread he gazed,
E'en while the sun in beauty blazed,
Till 'clipsed within that threatening cloud,
As 'twere within a sable shroud.
Like a fiery serpent wildly flew,
Adown the heavens the lightnings blue.
Hark! a burst of thunder deep and far,
As the war-drum's note, or the clattering car,
And many an ominous sound was heard
With the stormy petrel, that fearful bird,
Lashed by wild circumambient waves,
Oft plunged the barque to ocean caves.
The liquid thunders of the deep
Were summons dread of dreamless sleep;
From the sea-green gulf the ship emerged,
As o'er her masts broke the angry surge,
While o'er the waters inky face,
The white foam sailed like ghosts in chase.
Fast did the gaping billows rise,
Like mountains lifted to the skies,
O'er which the ship as in mad spasm,
Roll'd on and down the mighty chasm;
Then prayerful cries died on the startled air,

With curses hoarse, and wailings of despair,
'Twas vain,—lost was the ship—their doom was
    cast;
One mad'ning shriek rose on the yelling blast;
Then all went down with bubbling roar—
The stately bark and crew to rise no more!
Now floats the wreck in ocean spray,
And the moaning surges murmur—where are they?

THE GRADUATE'S FAREWELL.

When will ye think of me my friends?
When will ye think of me?—Hemans.

Farewell! my classmates—here's my hand,
    Tears are around my heart,
Thick crowding thoughts are thronging up,
    In this sad hour we part.

Patient we've trod the classic hall,
    Together day by day;
Where science on the dark'nd mind,
    Pours her celestial ray.

Together at the shrine of truth,
    We've bent with toil and pain;
Together spent the wealth of youth
    In learning's sacred fane.

And oft has midnight's weary hour,
    Bedim'd the radient eye,
As we the musty page explored;
    Nay, do not heave a sigh.

For when the daily task was o'er,
    In circles we have met;
To spend in mirth the rosy hours—
    Those hours shall we forget?

Nay brother—do not turn away,
    There's sadness on thy brow;
Now gird thee up the manly heart,
    'Tis life's commencement now.

Hark! a silvery voice—say, dost thou hear?
    It is the trump of fame;
Its notes come ringing sweet and clear,
    And sings a deathless name.

Then nerve thy arm and bare thy brow,
    To meet the world's dark strife,
And proudly breast the gales that blow,
    Amid the storms of life.

Thy noble energy of soul,
    Shall not be spent in vain;
The world shall feel the strong control
    Which minds like thine maintain.

In truth ye are a gallant band,
    My heart exults with pride;

As proudly beautiful ye stand
  Together by my side

THE MOON.

To Fazio.

> Beholding thee,
> Thou beauteous moon, forgotten passages,
> In the writ pages of life's volume come
> To me afresh, and thoughts of dim years past,
> Move in the soul.—*S. C. Kinney.*

When comes the solemn twilight hour,
  With noiseless step and sombre shade,
'Tis then I feel a wizzard power—
  A sadness soft my breast pervade.

And then the moon, so coldly bright,
  Lends sweet enchantment to the scene;
Sheds forth a flood of holy light,
  O'er stirless wood and vale serene.

Sweet friend, did ne'er her silvery face,
  Fair images to thee recall?
On memory's page, didst ne'er retrace
  The past—with its sad changes all?

The pale round moon—'tis still the same,
  As when Chaldean Shepherd swains,

With flocks and herds oft grazing came,
    Beneath her ray on Shinar's plains.

The same as when the Moslem came,
    Beneath her crescent pale and wan,
Razing each tower and Christian fane,
    Of powerful Byzantium.

E'en now she's looking sadly down,
    Upon those lonely solitudes;
Where marble columns—sculphtur'd stone,
    Lie scattered round in fragments rude.

Where once Palmyra's haughty queen,
    Zenobia—led in golden chains;
Through Roman streets was sadly seen,
    Conquer'd by proud Aurelian.

How much of joy, of woe and crime,
    Are conjur'd up beneath her face—
Wrote on the mildew page of time,
    As backward, thought, those scenes retrace.

But Fazio, when again the moon
    Upon thee sheds her mellow light,
Look on her, and then think of one,
    Who too may gaze with fond delight.

To an Absent One.

"From the bright stars, or from the viewless air,
 Or from some world unreach'd by human tho't,
Spirit, sweet spirit, if thy home be there,
 And if thy visions with the past be fraught,
  Answer me—answer me!"—*Hemans*

From friends, and home, and native land,
 Thy roving feet have stray'd;
From proud Miami's classic band
 And academic shade,
  Where art thou, where?

Oh! tell us, on what sunny isle,
 Thy far off home is made?
Thou take'st from our hearth the smile,
 That was too bright to fade.
  Where art thou, where?

Dwell'st thou by the sounding shore,
 Where swift the blue waves curl;
Amid the ocean's deaf'ning roar,
 Where ships their sails unfurl?
  Not there.

Or wand'rest where the ice-berge gleams,
 Deep fus'd in sunset dyes;
Where the ocean eagle soaring screams,
 Earth's tidings to the skies?
  Not there.

Where many a royal Saxon tower,
    Upvaults with glit'ring dome ;
O'er broad Sarmatia—land of power,
    Of toiling serfs the home ?
        Not there.

Shall we find thee on the Alpine hills,
    Or glaciers icy plains ?
Where oft the huntsman's clarion shrill,
    Breaks forth in gladsome strains ?
        Not there.

Do'st linger in those southern shades,
    The land of fadeless flow'rs ?
In sweet Arcadia's sunny glades,
    Or Andalusian bowers ?
        Not there.

Tell us ye spirits of earth and sky,
    Doth the lov'd one dwell in a world more fair ?
Where the heart hath no grief, and the bosom no sight,
    Spirit, sweet spirit ! if thy home be there,
        Answer me ! answer me.

Low voices like the sound of streams,
    Far off—through the cold still air
Respond, and through my dreams,
    Mournfully answer—where ?
        O ! where ?

To Leonore.

> What now to her is all the world esteems?
> She is awake, and cares not for its dreams,
> But moves while yet on earth as one above,
> Its hopes and fears, its loathing and its loves.
> Crabbe.

It is the hour of night's still solemn noon,
And the heaven-encircled earth is wrapt in slumber;
While through the glittering isles of light the absent moon,
Sheds no pelucid beam amid the number
Of golden spheres ; nor clouds, nor vaporous stains encumber,
Their silent walks along the dark blue plains;
And through the shades of night, cold, calm and sombre,
Glides soft lip't silence o'er the world again,
Stealing earth's children from their toil and pain.

Lone watcher of the night, art thou Leonore; no beam
Responsive, from sympathetic eyes now tells
Its love, or shines into thy heart, save the gleam
Of the clear cold eyes of night, and it would seem
Upon thy spirit hung pale melancholy's spell,
Coloring with misty doubts and fears each hope-born dream;
While solitude with all her musing children dwell,
Around thy hearth, with brooding thoughts such as we may not tell.

It is no sudden change that prays upon thy mind,

But a deep sense of utter loneliness;
A solitude of soul—a grief refined,
O! naught that's earthly now thy heart can bless,
Nor song of hope—nor loves deep tenderness—
Thine is not a common woe—in tears
It finds no outlet; they could not express,
Thine inward sorrow, which corrodes and sears,
For it hath lain upon thy heart and burnt for years.

Beat on great heart of time! beat on, beat on,
Thou hast no balsam for the spirit's wound,
Nor can'st thou e'er recall the priceless things now gone,
The golden chain is rent which all so sweetly bound,
With garlands fair the future may be crown'd,
And yet they ne'er can wear the rosy bloom,
Of those that gem the past—now strown around,
Earth's changes pale have shrouded them in gloom,
Stern destiny forever seal'd thy doom.

And thou amidst the reckless crowd dost wander,
Seeking some lethean draught for thy heart's woe,
And tho' thou seem'st familiar, still thou art a stranger,
For none the fearful depth's of thy heart's griefs may
    know,
Lip and knee worshipers are there, in accents low,
Breathing sweet words, and flatteries vain,
Who, for the weak weave snares—but oh!
'Tis discord to thine ears, and to thy heart 'tis pain:
They do but mock the things, that ne'er may be again.

(c)

Remember'st thou thy youthful halcyon days,
When high-born hope did thy pure soul inspire
When thou with careless fingers oft essay'd
To wake the latent music of some spirit lyre?
Seldom came sounds harmonious from those mysterious
    wires,
Harsh dissonance and jarring discord fell
Only upon thy silvery ear—there glows no fire,
Of angel poesy in minds impure, or dwell
Sweet heavenly thoughts which oft in music swell.

Yet midst thy lonely wanderings thou hast swept,
One sacred harp, to whose wild strings thou hast bent
In list'ning fear, hoping some tone to have kept
In memory's ear. Alas! its strains are spent,
The spirit sounds are dead—the chords are rent,
The gush of melody—the full deep tone—
Is hush'd; yet faint and low thy sorrowing song is blent,
With the evening winds, whose hollow moan,
Seems like some spirit's voice in answer to thine own

A change is in thy song, sweet Leonore;
'Tis like the bulbul's lonely wail when heard,
Where pale young roses weep when day is o'er,
Beneath the orient moon, sweet mournful bird;
Yet must forgetfulness—oh! painful word,—
Spread like a funeral pall her sable veil,
Over the past, which ne'er may be disturbed
By memories sad, alas! 'twould naught avail,
To waste thy music in a funeral wail.

How like a tissuey woof, how wonderful is mind!
How with each fibrous thought one idea dear,
May like a golden thread these thoughts together bind;
While pale distrust, and hope, and quivering fear,
With trembling, and dismay, and burning tears,
With clear brow'd confidence wage open war,
To rend that band away—while fate severe,
With flaming sword presents a fearful bar,
To the soft beams of hope's auspicious star.

Music.

Addressed to a Listener.

And thou didst stay thy steps; did'st linger nigh,
And wherefore? A careless list'ner was't thou,
Unto my wild untutor'd lays—my rustic songs?
Or is thy soul like mine?—ever as a stream,
Which gushing flows away in gentle sounds?
What said those wind-waked melodies to thee?
Or did their lowly breathings fail to reach thine heart?
Did not those gentle tones inspire thee with a sense
Most sweet of heaven and its celestial bliss?
While of the palmy bowers of Paradise,
Thou had'st a bright and joyous dream?
Methinks while bending o'er my simple harp,
Some gentle seraph on my throbbing breast

Had laid his hand and whispered, peace be still,
While all the warring passions hush'd to rest
As soft as those within an infant's breast,
In quiet slept.

What tho' sad memories
May darkly revel in the woe-worn soul,
With many bitter griefs and sorrows fraught?
What though remembrance of the world's dark strife,
May press upon the aching and the weary heart,
Yet music can the wounded spirit soothe,
In memories soft, as summer evening's latest sigh.
I knew that thou wert near, and tremulous grew my
    hand;
Why, I could not tell—but all in vain I strove,
Those spirit stirring harmonies to wake
Once more—when a sweet wand'ring sprite,
Swept by, and with a silvery wing soft touch'd
My mute and saddened harp—and sweet a strain,
Of melody gush'd forth, to the glad songs
Of Paradise akin, or rather like
Some exiled angel's lay—breathing a sad lament,
That earth-born joys are but fantastic fever-dreams.

Song of the Sprite.

Wake, mortal wake!
  Awake from thy dreaming;
Lean not on earth,
  All is but seeming;

Earth has no joy,
　　Unshaded by sorrow,
Spring's fairest flowers
　　Will fade on the morrow.

And what is man's goodness?
　　Mix'd with weakness and folly
And the sound of his life,
　　Is a tone melancholy:
Thou art but dust,
　　A mutable creature;
Thy affections bestow not,
　　On weak human nature.

Then wake, mortal wake,
　　Awake from thy dreaming,
Lean not on earth,
　　All is but seeming.

A most delicious softness on my spirit fell,
While the sweet joy of grief, a trembling tear,
Had gathered, and on my drooping eyelids hung,
And yet I was not sad, but 'twas a joy most sweet,
So near allied are all the joys and griefs
Of earth, that both in their excess,
Are fraught with tears—entranc'd I listened,
And I fancied that the evening wind did sob,
As with a dying fall the fairy breathings ceased.
My heart which had grown still now throbbed again.
I turned me round—the fairy sprite had flown,
While silently thou had'st departed too.

Lines

On the death of a Lady who died on the eve of her departure for her paternal home.

A sufferer on a sick-bed lay,
    Around whose aching head,
Dread fever-fires in rage made way,
    Whence reason's light had fled.

'Twas but a few short days before,
    A babe sat on her knee;
And as she softly murmur'd o'er,
    A mother's minstrelsy:
Sweet haunting thoughts blent with the strain,
    And hopeful visions bright,
That those she loved might yet again,
    Smile on her gladdened sight.

Alas! the long, long, wish'd for day,
    Beamed o'er the blooming earth,
While she upon her death-couch lay,
    Far from the household hearth;
The fever plague alas! had set
    Its hectic on her cheek—
With clammy dews her brow was wet,
    Her voice was low and weak.

And did she then that hope forget?
    With which her dreams were fraught—

Say, did sweet mem'ry linger yet,
  Within that fane of thought?
Ah! yes—throughout her fever-dreams,
  That ceaseless wish had sway,
As falls on dark benighted streams,
  Some lonely planet's ray.

And thus the suff'er sadly spoke,
"Say are we not most there?"
And from some startling dream awoke,
"Where are my sisters, where?"
"Oh! yes; we'll be there by and by,"
  With warm and anxious friends,
While o'er her couch with mournful eyes,
  An anxious watcher bends.

"We're almost there—we're almost there"
  Again she feebly said—
"I see the wild streams flashing fair,
  O'er many a rock-bound bed."
Oh! there in innocence I've play'd,
  And rear'd the beechen bow'r,
And down the flow'ry dell have stray'd
  In childhood's elfin hour.

But all at once the voice was still,
  The pulses ceas'd their play;
The longing dream was now fulfill'd,
  In yon bright world away;
And seraphs from the realms of light,

Bent o'er the dying bed,
While on their wavering pinions bright,
Her grieving spirit fled.

Oh! she indeed had found the goal,
A blissful home at last;
Beyond—where time's dark surges roll,
The weary soul had pass'd.
No more along her father's hall,
Shall sound her parting words,
Or ringing laugh, or light foot-fall,
Or voice so like a bird's.

Call it not hard that she hath gone,
Beyond our aching sight;
Upon her soul a glorious dawn,
Bursts forth in floods of light,
For life is but a passing dream,
A ray—a dim uncertain gleam,
Of joys beyond the tomb.

Life's toiling transient day is done,
The spirit's mission o'er;
Substantial life it hath begun,
Where it had bloom'd before.
We know that thou art happy there,
In thy celestial rest,
In angel robes thou'lt wax more fair,
With those the pure and bless'd.

Where fadeless bowers immortal wav
   Dost thou remember still?
Or did'st in lethean waters lave,
   And quaff thy spirit's fill?
Say, wil't thou from thy natal skies,
   Or some sweet starry sphere,
Bend earth-ward, still thy radient eye
   Watch o'er the lov'd ones here?

'Tis silent all—and evening shades,
   Are sadly gathering round;
A mournful joy my breast pervades;
   Some spell my heart hath bound.
And now I hear the autumn winds
   Wail through the perish'd leaves—
That sound in thee a semblance finds,
   So mournfully it grieves.

And as the sobbing voice floats by
   With deep and solemn swell,
To weeping flow'rs it seems to sigh
   A spirit's sad farewell!

The Daguerrean Gallery.

  Let's call and see the pictures—
A fairy grot, this gallery of art!
Where true to life, and nature pictur'd stand,
  Groupings and forms, that facinate the heart;
So perfect is this skill the master can command.

  The old, the young are there,
And bright amid the galaxy of faces,
Is one with fair young brow and eyes serene,
  The child of love and favor'd of the graces,
Of all the throng, the " star particular," and queen.

  Look on this picture here—
Is it not like?—else wherefore flow my tears?
Oh! yes—too true; this faithful semblance dear,
  Of one he lov'd thro' dark and shad'wy years,
A wand'rer in the groves of some supernal sphere.

  And here as in thy life—
The same arch smile around thy lip is playing,
The tender radience of thy fervent eyes,
  As when on happy scenes their gaze was straying,
And soft their light as beams of midnight skies.

  And on thy open brow,
In careless grace a wealth of sunny hair,
Is clustering still, in many a wavelet fair,
  Aye; all are there—each feature of that face divine!
Oh! genius bright, the power, the gift is thine.

Oh! art mysterious—
That with thy heav'n-born hand-maid light can'st
    trace,
The image of the mind in form and face,
Which impress on the spotless page shall last,
Preserved from blight or mould till time is past.

The Pen.

Come gentle muse, in measur'd lays once more,
Unto the penman's art thy votive offerings pour;
Come let us roam along the aisles of time,
By Zion's sacred streams and hills sublime;
Where once of old with soul and mind inspir'd,
An ancient scribe with heaven's wisdom fir'd,
On Parian tablets white as artic snow,
The sacred law transcribed—and hence we know—
The pen's great art is sacred and divine!
Since he who formed our being's grand design,
First wrought with holy hand the skiey lore,
That all the nations worship and adore.

And by this hallow'd Book are we not told
Of Babalonia's king, who, in the days of old
His lordly guests unto a royal feast
Had summon'd; and richest viands of the east,
With priceless treasures from the temple brought,

Shone on the board by cunning workmen wrought.
And when the stirring voice of revelry went high,
And sounds of harp and lute, with voices soft swept by,
Amid the rosy splendors of Belshazzar's pillar'd halls,
While sweet aromas rose along the gilded walls.

Over against the lamps a shad'wy hand did glide,
Which, when the king beheld, his heart within him died.
Trembling and pale, convulsed and fix'd he sate,
As blasted by a spell, with eyes of fear and hate,
A stifled cry arose as if the monarch dream'd,
While from his burning gaze remorse and madness
    gleam'd;
Stony and cold his brow as when in death's repose,
Around the writhing heart its icy waters close.
God's finger wrote his doom, high on the gorgeous wall,
And morning red beheld the impious tyrant's fall.

And what the triumphs that the pen hath wrought;
That herald of the heart, and mercury of thought.
Lo! when a little band of valient men,
Proclaimed "we will be free"—the wing'd pen
Swept o'er the spotless page—a glorious word
Impress'd—and when the old world wondering heard,
Proud Albion's Lion roar'd in thunder tones,
And orient despots trembled on their thousand thrones.
Beyond the western wave an empire rose,
O'er which the olive's fragrant blossoms close;
Where   om's eagle builds her eyrie wild,

And wraps her " œgis" round her free-born child.
The pen hath spoken! and not all in vain,
The bloodless sword, that hath its thousands slain,
The potent instrument of genius-gifted minds;
The wizzard power—the mystic link that binds
The glittering gems that grace the labyrinths of time.
How varied are its powers—how low, yet how sublime,
" To build the lofty verse, or honied lines of rhyme,
To blazon evil deeds or consecrate a crime."

 Now twined with cypress boughs, or laurel wreaths
Of love, and hope, and fame, and death it breathes,
With thoughts that through the soul's deep sanctum's
  thrill,
To soothe the aching heart, or bind the tameless will.
Doth not our hearts exult, grow still—expire?
As o'er the poet's page of breathing fire,
Instinct with soul and mind, when rapt we learn,
Those living truths that shall forever burn?
And by its aid the volume of the past,
Unto a wondering world has been unseal'd,
While stripp'd of dust and blight now stand revealed
The glories of the old Augustan age,
Of hero, warrior-bard and poet-sage.
Mark! with what skill the artist can combine,
With written charm and talismanic sign,
The chaste, the smoothe, the graceful and refin'd,
In characters of thought that syllable the mind,
Who would not learn with strength and ease to wield,

This weapon of the mind in learning's boundless field?
Who would not emulate the master's art,
That facinates the eye and speaks unto the heart?
Whose nimble pen glides through the wordy chase,
With many a circling curve or line of waving grace.
Thus far I have proceeded with my theme
As through the tissuey windings of a dream,
And yet not half the spoils are counted o'er,
Brought by the pen down time's benighted shore,
Not half the triumph's by its influence won,
Since light and truth, their high career begun.
Yet, if my humble lay, unto this sacred art,
An influence lends, that speaks to mind and heart,
My wishes are achieved—my object won,
The muse's task is ended and my song is done.

CHILDHOOD'S RAMBLES.

"Sweetly wild, sweetly wild,
  Were the scenes that charmed me when a child."

Happiest was I in childhood's day,
  Wand'ring among the early flowers of May;
    By streams of sweetest trill,
    In the slant shades of evening still,
    Along the hedge-grown paths;
Or o'er the fields where, wending on his way,

Amid the fragrant swaths
Of new made hay;
The merry plow-boy sings his careless lay.
Or staying at rosy morn',
Amid the gentle flocks—
Their snowy fleeces shorn;
Nipping the low sweet shrubs that grow.
O'er moss-grown rocks,
And ledges steep;
Where groups of virgin snow-drops peep,
And green the pendant ivy creeps,
In the black silence of the glen,
Where all day long,
The damps among,
The moody owl sleeps.
These are the scenes that charmed me then.
And oft in childhood,
Through the wild wood,
Where the fragrant woodbine blows
With the single petal'd rose;
I sought the spring,
In steep banks hidden,
Whose waters constant gush unbidden;
Or cool down dripping,
The green rocks o'er;
While distant roar,
Of cascade wild,
Sweetly charmed me when a child.
Or wending among the golden shocks,

Of dew-perfuming grain,
Sweet as the breath of early rain,
Where groups of stalwart men,
With mirth and jocund songs again;
  In scant frocks
  Of flaxen woof,
  The hospitable roof
  At early morn forsake,
And in the labors of the field partake.
And where tassel'd corn,
With rich lands of fresh plow'd ground,
 Yield fragrance to the summer air;
  While welcome sound
  Of supper horn,
Bade from the field the rustic swain repair.
 Or rambling along the plain,
 Alone throughout the live long day;
  Humming some wild strain,
  Of self-taught roundelay;
  By fence rows far,
 That skirt some distant field,
Or loitering late when bright the vesper star,
 Shines from afar as would a silver shield;
  And bearing home the spoils,
  Of childhood's rambles;
With quick and stealthy step along the brake,
  Where hidden coils,
  The fear-awakening snake;
  Or trilling oft a merry lay,

And timing it with buoyant step and childish gambol,
Thoughtless I sought my home-directed way.
With wreaths of heart's ease white and blue;
My bosom's own peculiar flower,
That in the nooks and corners of the fence rows grew
Or from some woody height or lowly bower,
The box-wood's feathry bloom;
With string'd buds in scarlet strans,
Woven in shining bands;
Gleeful o'er my young brows thrown,
And with the loose locks careless worn,
That darkly strayed in childish grace,
Around a pensive face.
And on my way star-lit,
Oft seeking leaves of fungi race;
Orange and scarlet,
Wrought in gay festoon;
Where mimic orchard's grew of white mushroom,
With velvet mosses;
And feathery fern its pliant stamen tosses,
To the soft daliance of the waving breeze;
And with the wealth of these,
Grouping among translucent water weeds,
Like stringed beads;
Bright prism-colored shells,
Those water sounding bells,
Within whose radient cells,
With voice most soft,
Some fairy oft

Full many a tale of ocean tells.
And reach'd the orchard's wealth of snowy bloom,
　　Where with perfume,
　　My youthful sense grew glad;
　　A joy so sweet—yet sad—
Thus all the joys I ever knew,
　　Were tinged with that peculiar hue,
　　Of pleasant gloom;
　　Like roses blooming o'er a tomb.
I sought where mid the apple boughs,
　　And snow-white blows,
Hid by a woof of dark green leaves;
　　Blithe robin red-breast,
　　In dark brown vest,
His feathered temple weaves;
　　In sooth I thought
　　The builder bird
A fairy net-work wrought,
　　Of rarest masonry.
　　And when I heard,
　　His sky born melody,
That like a flood of rippling sound,
　　Woke all the echoes round;
　　While sporting in the sunset's glow,
　　My youthful wonder sought to know,
　　Whence without control,
　　Did those gleeful numbers roll,
　　That he would pour with all his soul?
Sang he of distant goal,

Or memory-cherished climes;
  Where softest chimes,
Of music-murmuring streams,
  Fall on the ear a 'transing sound;
  And where like starry beams,
  Or snow flakes falling round:
  The beauteous bridal rose,
  In tender fragrance blows?
But childhood's sinless hours are gone,
  Its dreams forever fled;
The bird from apple bough has flown,
  And the happy scene is speed:
For I've left the haunts that my childhood knew,
  And the silent distances of blue;
Full many a veil of tissuey hue,
  Have cast o'er weary leagues between,
  And shut from sight the haunting scene.

A Portrait.

Aye; it is fair, e'en as the brow of night's
Pale regent, whose enchanted beams stole down,
The Latmian hills of old, and charm'd
Endymeon's heart to joy and paphean dreams.

Upon that pale young brow bright intellect
Sits enthrone'd—where glowing thought oft breaks
Its deep repose, those azure eyes illume.
And on the parian forehead smooth and white,

In gentle dalliance with the wooing winds,
Now float in careless grace soft silken locks
Of jetty hair; while round the classic mouth,
A smile as pleasant as the looks of angels'
Lingers still. And through those lit eyes come
From the far holy of the soul's pure deeps,
Those clear translucent floods of spirit-light
E'en as the stars—are pure, and beautifully bright.
While over all a mournful beauty hangs,
A pensive joy—like to the mellow gloom,
That round the lofty woods sad autumn casts.
And yet these varied charms with conscious pride are
    blent,
Which on that brow as nobly sits,
As would a god upon a skyey throne!
Oh! 'tis a face love fain would recollect,
And memory clasp as with a circean spell;
The enraptur'd soul of Phidias would glow
With inspirations new and beautiful,
Could he but gaze upon those lineaments divine;
And all of which dear friend, are purely, truly thine.

GENIUS.

Celestial gift! thy light is cast around afar,
Like the etherial blaze of an undying star

From age to age thine influence pure is given,
Oh! thou of powers divine; fair child of heaven!
Wandering alone, along the halls of time,
In this our mundane sphere—life's transcient clime.
  Thou com'st methinks, on holy mission sent,
With patient zeal and most sublime intent,
Around thy shrine in willing homage bows,
A wond'ring world, while round thy lofty brows
Are twined bright laurel wreaths of fame,
Whose clarion tones proclaim a deathless name.
  But who amid earth's multitudes can comprehend,
The mighty striving of thy spirit—or shall blend
Their souls with thine?—there is no second self
Thy thoughts to mirror back—shall sordid pelf,
Lean avarice—self-loving interest, and worldly gains,
Forever all absorb men's hearts, and souls, and
    brains?
Alas! for thee, oh, genius!—'tis thy peculiar lot,
Ne'er to be wholy known, or e'er forgot—
A voice methinks I hear from distant ages,
Have ye not heard of it, oh! ye bards and sages?
Upon the soul it flings a dreamy spell,
Mournful and strange as the sound farewell;
Yet are its tones prophetic—they seem to sigh
Alone, alone; as if thy destiny—
In solemn grandeur wrapt and pleasing gloom,
Was told in those sad words of doom.
Ah! strangely fearful words—they will express
Of all thy woes the cause—earth-sickness and distress.

Hark! that voice—as from the past I hear its solemn
    tone,
" Link divine; 'twixt Deity and man, live thou alone!"
Proud in the isolation of thy soul,
Art thou, oh, Genius! Where is thy spirit's goal?
No sympathies there are to bind thee to the earth,
In this our twilight being, there is a chilly dearth
Of thought and feeling—there is no spirit-ear
Amidst the multitude like thine, attun'd to hear
The silvery music of each glittering sphere,
Or whisper'd melodies of the eternal thought,
With which the rushing winds and roaring storms are
    fraught;
No mental eyes to see the things that burn,
In the fair radiance of truth, which thy clear eyes
    discern,
Fearfully gifted is this child of heaven,
Wrestling to fulfill his mighty mission given;
Of all shades of feeling—his life is a story
From lowest shame, to loftiest glory.
He hath drained the fountains of all earthly lore,
And yet, unsatisfied in soul, still sighs for more;
And oft in his sweet dreamy musing hours,
He stoops to hear the silent hymn of dreaming
    flowers,
Then soars on spirit wings beyond each shining star,
From whence his sacred lore and wisdom comes afar.
From the conflicting interests of mankind apart,
He hath composed in his scant garret a brief chart,

Of love and death, and hope, and fame—'tis life's
    history,
A dark, yet glorious, sublime and subtle mystery.
    With stately step he comes through the long night
Of ages dead where wept its mildew blight;
Dark superstition, that topas of the mind,
Wrapt in his thoughts stupendous—amid'st mankind
Is heard his seer-like voice—his immortal songs
Have broke the night of ignorance which long
Hung like an incubus upon the minds of men,
Chasing the sombre clouds away, as when
Aurora blushes at the gates of morning skies
In rosy splendors.
              No more shall despots rise,
To chain his struggling spirit—what though their links
    may bind
His free-born limbs—the fetterless mind,
O'er leaping earth, borne on the wings of thought shall
    soar
Back to its native realm, where long before,
Bloom'd the pure soul in everlasting day,
Ere yet its spirit-wings had pass'd away.
Hence his dreams of a brighter existence,
Of boundless glories beyond the distance,
Of time and space where deathless bowers,
Weep dews immortal.
              By divinest powers,
Were not these radiant visions given him? Hence,

His lore intuitive and mystic wisdom. Hence,
His dreams of the soul's freedom for which he deeply
    longs,
Does he not breathe it in his plaining songs,
The inspiration that his soul had caught,
The power and lightning flashes of deep thought,
Gushed from the fountians of eternal truth,
Whose heavenly streams shall yield immortal youth.
Oh, light divine! what but for thee,
Must this dark world have been?—its misery
Hast thou not turn'd to joy and raised from gloom
Our hearts—strewing with flow'rs of hope the lethean
    tomb.
New tones thou'st given unto the spirit's lyre,
And brought from heaven its celestial fire,
Warming to light, and life, and loveliness the earth,
With form of ideal beauty and of heavenly birth.
    The tones majestic of great Milton's lyre,
Have we not heard, and felt our hearts grow still—
    expire?
When the immortal Handal and Mozart,
Pour'd their wild anthems o'er the Alpine hills,
Was there e'er one, who in his inmost heart,
By its wild throbbing and its burning thrill,
Felt not they were celestial and echoing still,
Through the blue deep from the far lyres of heaven,
It seem'd a concert by the seraphs given,
Born and dying at the mighty minstrel's will.

Thou speak'st, Oh, Genius! the heritors of ages
We become, as we unfold their mouldering pages,
The mists of time roll back, and the thick dust
Which on the noble dead had gathered with the rust
Of years, are scatter'd—and we feel within us burn
Our hearts, when we hear that in the urn
Of the hoary past lie heroes, martyrs, sages
Wrapt in the somber gloom of distant ages,
In mental vision do we not see them pass
Along the stream of time a glorious mass ;
The noblest part of life's fraternity,
Leaving a glory lasting as eternity.
Years lay dreamily and chill upon the past,
Enrapt in gloom a dark chaotic waste,
Until thou—oh! radient one, with visions bright,
Upon its ample page didst shed a light.
To thee, the past unfolds its mysteries,
And crumbling monuments, and histories
Of lost races—ruins of earth and thrones
Demolished—dynasties extinct—unknown
Nations, with all the giant wrecks of time,
Which still exist in every land and clime,
Have been from darkness and the engulphing past,
By thy superhuman power to light restored at last.
Majestic are thy works, oh, Genius! by thine aid,
Weeping humanity is comforted and staid.
Thou strik'st the lyre ; thy radient eyes,
Full of the mysticisms of the skies,
Beyond the rolling spheres is heavenward bent ;

While floating through thy mind are dim presentiment
Of a majestic destiny for all thy race,
When the glad earth shall rest in harmony and peace.
When order, from disorder shall have sprung,
And joy shall reign of which the angel's sung.
We hear thy burning songs, and now
We feel we are immortal—hast not thou
Link'd time with eternity? Chosen thou art
To enter the most holy place; thy great heart
Is full of inspiration, while to us is given,
A palmy joy—a living sense of heaven.
Nearer to earth seem its celestial plains,
As wrapt we listen to thy lofty strains,
Sublime and sweet as songs of Paradise,
When at Aurora's birth in orient skies,
Hesperus led the morning stars, whose song
Exulting broke the stillness of creation. Among
Yon wheeling orbs—the eternal music rings;
Genius, thou hearest, great interpreter of things
Most holy—by thy hand-maid Art we view
Images most fair, and of prismatic hue,
We feel a subtle spirit of delight
Transfuse our frames—visions of light
Dart through the mind, as oft we gaze
Upon the glorious arts of other days.
Moments there are when the impassion'd soul
Would burst its prison, and without control
Stretch forth its youthful wings, and hence
Clothed in aromal robes commence.

Angel; alas! 'tis but a phantasy—a dream;
A glimpse—a drop of the celestial dew,
That we have tasted—a joy intense and new.

THE WANDERING SHIP.

The following Poem was suggested by a notice in "Scott's Weekly Paper," of a ship, which, having been abandoned and set on fire, sailed the distance of two thousand miles without a man on board. She hailed from New Brunswick—was discovered off Cape Clear, and towed into Cork.

Lo! where upon the seas in outlines dim,
    Some spectral form begirt with feathery spray;
Along the horizon's encircling rim,
    Floats proudly on its solitary way.

But look again! as nearer still it glides,
    A stately barque now meets the yearning view;
How gracefully the billowy deep she rides,
    Through veils of wreathing fog and vapors blue.

Proudly aloft her towering masts arise,
    And yet no helms-man bold, or pilot brave,
Or flowing sails, now greet our wondering eyes—
    No signal colors from her mast-head wave.

" No dread alarms on the rent air float,"
    Or shouts of woe, or wailings of despair;

No booming gun, or soul-awakening note,
   Of warning bell—all, all is silent there.

And yet how lightly—buoyantly she sweeps,
   Across the wildering waste of waters drear;
As doth a bird that cleaves ethereal deeps,
   No hand to guide, no eye to steer.

Or like some lone and isolated soul,
   Without or friends or home, striving to gain
Some island heaven of rest, some peaceful goal,
   'Midst the cold surges of life's dark domain.

A fearful, pleasing sight, that silent barque,
   As nearer, yet more near, she draws to view;
Abandoned to the surging billows dark,
   Bereft—alone to stray without a crew.

Why alone and tenantless go'st thou forth?
   Tell us, what secrets doth thy breast contain;
To the ice mountains of the rock-bound north,
   Art bound thou barque? or to the southern main?

But look within; what meets the startled sight?
   Ruin hath left its awful impress there;
'Tis dark and silent as a moonless night,
   And looks a very symbol of despair.

Who hath wrought this deed of desolation?
   And whither have thy wretched inmates flown?
Here havoc sits enthroned—and desolation

Hovers round; yield, oh, barque! some answering
    tone.

Who hath despoiled thee of thy treasures vast?
    Thy gold and gems, and trappings beautiful?
Thy streamers proud, that round about thy masts
    Waved to the ocean breeze?—thy blacken'd hull.

In chilling gloom responds; methinks thou'st roam'd
    O'er many a weary league of ocean;
Where foam-plum'd waves, and spray-wreath'd
    breakers comb'd
Thy lonely deck, while to the beck'ning motion

Of the seas thou'st bent, and then there came
    Annihilation grim with torch of fire;
And on thy gorgeous walls in blasting flame,
    Its devastation left—yet could not tire.

Thy struggling frame. fiercer and wilder still,
    As if to mock the progress of decay;
The blight swept on—and yet o'er many a hill
    Of flashing brine, thy noble prow made way.

And plunging waves did goad thy creaking sides,
    Banners of flame were round about thee furl'd;
Yet gallantly thou'st faced the roaring tides,
    To roam alone o'er ocean's shad'way world.

Thou'st boldly rode before the whirlwind's wrath,
    And heeded not the thunder-trumpet's blaze;

Nor raging elements in their battle-path,
  And bid defiance to the lightning's glare

Then speed thee on, thou wand'rer of the deep,
  With naught to cheer before, or weep behind;
Thy haven, the waves, where silver moon-beams sleep,
  Thy realm, the sea—thy sails, the winged wind.

Thy comrades–things, that in thy wake shall play,
  Thy voices, sounds—that in the breakers dwell,
And as they bare thy less'ning form away,
  Do seem to moan in haunting tones—farewell!

THE MANIAC.

" Such things are."

Hark! that wild shriek—'tis borne upon the gale,—
It is a frenzied maiden's fearful wail;
That voice which oft gush'd forth in sweetest song,
In broken tones now trembling floats along;
She comes—behold her—fading—dying,
Her withered hopes around her lying,
Her care-worn cheek now faded grown,
Whose roses are forever flown.
The vacant gaze of that wild eye,
The unsubdued and deep drawn sigh,

The transcient flush upon her cheek,
The clenched hands—the piercing shriek,
The dark brown hair dishevel'd now,
With straw wreath twin'd around her brow,
Her rounded form—her graceful air,
Now wan and wasted by despair,
Tells of a dark and deadly strife,
Within her breast destroying life.
Now seldom does the tear drop start,
Tho' grief is wasting her young heart;
Scorched is her brain by phrenzy's fire,
Quench'd in her heart each young desire.
Gone is that light elastic tread,
Which scarcely bent the violet's head;
Her taper fingers in despair,
She mingles with her flowing hair,
She plucks and gives it to the wind,
(Fit emblem of her tortured mind,)
Which oft through haunted church-yard raves,
In fitful gusts o'er mouldering graves.
And, as in Spring young tender flowers,
Oft droop beneath the weight of showers,
Like them she droops the vales along,
And sings anon a plaintive song.
E'en now I hear her phrenzied laugh,
She's deeply drank of sorrow's draught;
Upon the startled air it rings,
And now she laughs—and now she sings—
It tells to me in language sad,

Poor child of sorrow, thou art mad :—

Song.

They call me crazed and simple maid,
    And ask me why I roam ;
And me they cruelly upbraid,
    As oft they hear me moan.

They ask me why my pensive song,
    When heard at eve is sad ;
They hint that I have suffer'd wrong,
    But then—I am not mad.

'Tis true this riven heart of mine,
    Will never more be glad ;
That here in loneliness I pine,
    But then—I am not mad.

I'm weary of the sounds of life,
    My brain is hot—my heart is sore ;
When will the mad'ning fever strife
    Of my rent heart be o'er ?

Sweet as the notes of the dying swan,
In mournful melody glides on—
That voice—attun'd in happier days,
To trembling strings or saphic lays ;
But now she starts as from a dream,
I hear her weep, and sob, and scream,
She sings again, all wild and shrill,

It echoes over vale and hill:—

Song.

I hear the scream of the mountain bird,
    And the howling storm at sea;
And the shriek of the mighty winds are heard
    Far o'er the distant lea.

The harsh and grating thunders roll,
    Along yon mountain crag;
But wilder horrors wreck my soul,
    As me they downward drag,

A curse is on my wither'd heart,
    A sleepless eye is mine;
I pray that I may soon depart,
    And woe and care resign.

The deep'ning shades of twilight fall,
And spread around a sable pall;
Forth comes the moon in vapory shroud,
Adown the sky through mist and cloud,
And now her shining forehead laves,
In the clear serene of ocean waves.
The Maniac's voice is hush'd and past,
She wanders forth amid the blast,
Where the raven cries and the owlets scream,
'Neath the glim'ring stars that faintly gleam,
She grasps within her hand a steel,
" This—this shall all my sorrows heal."

(D)

Then with a wild and shriek-like laugh,
She snaps the fatal blade in half,
" Away "—she cries—" thou deathful blade "—
And flings it to the adjacent glade.

  * * * * *

She starts—that wild and bloodshot eye,
Is turned upon the earth—the sky—
" Welcome "—she cries—" thou deep, deep sea,
" My wasted form I'll hide in thee ;"
Then with a madden'd voice she cried
Of fell despair and grief allied,
" Ye cavern'd spirits of the earth,
" Come forth with all your fiendish mirth,
" Ye're not more fearful in your arts,
" Than the fell purposes of men's hearts,
" O ! bear me to some Lethean wave,
" Where wretched spirits cease to rave,
" Exult ye in my sorrows dire,
" I shall not feel your vengeful ire."
Her voice grew weak—its piercing tone,
Now sank into a plaintive moan :
" Ye spirits of yon starry realm,
" My soul, which now sad griefs o'erwhelm,
" Receive, and let it cleansed be,
" From earth-born follies ever free,
" Possess'd of new develop'd powers,
" Roaming through Amaranthine bowers,
" Through azure fields, I'd soar afar,
" Through the cold moon-beams from star to star,

" On wings of silvery light I'd fly,
" Through the rainbow arches of the sky,
" Where flaming worlds in ether glow,
" And Truth's celestial fountains flow.
" Beyond those orbs of golden ray
" Through trackless space I'd wing my way,
" Till I reach'd the viewless gates of heaven,
" Where I might rest and be forgiven.
  * * * * *
Sure now some direful purpose she intends,
As o'er the rocky cliff she bends;
She flings her wasted arms on high,
While dark despair gleams in her eye:
" Welcome sweet sea! in thy oblivious wave,
" My fevered brow and faded form I'll lave."
A sudden plunge—one shriek—the scene is o'er—
The wretched maiden is no more.
Amazed the startled water nymphs survey'd
The stranger who thus dar'd their halls invade,
And music from her pearly shell
Peal'd forth a deep and solemn knell,
The melody of chiming waters flow'd,
From rocky steeps to dismal depths below,
And the sullen roar of the dashing surge,
Sent forth in leaden sounds a dirge,
The Tritons mourned and the Naids wept,
While the maid in their crystal bowers they kept,
The Mermaid braided her glossy hair,
With her cold damp fingers; long and fair,

Her tears congeal'd to strings of pearl,
With which she entwin'd each clustering curl,
With a coral wreath she bound her head,
And laid her on an amber bed;
With a diamond clasp she bound her hands,
And cover'd her o'er with golden sands—
And thus the Mermaid wept and sang,
While sweet through the ocean-halls it rang.
Hark! hear her song, 'tis as sweet and low
As the Nymphs' who sing in the sunset's glow.
" Thou art laid in thy silent chamber low,
" Where the flower-like gems of ocean grow.
" Sleep on—within our crystal cell,
" May soft-winged peace around thee dwell."
And thus the Mermaid sang and wept,
While calmly and deeply the maiden slept.
The demi-gods breath'd from their tinted shell,
To the death-cold maid a long farewell:
" Now soft and sweet is the maiden's sleep,
" In tears no more shall her eyelids steep;
" Thou art lull'd forever to sweet repose
" By the rocking waves that over thee close;
" May the wrecking of ships, and the mariner's screams,
" Disturb not thy long night with troublous dreams;
" May memory's echo never fall,
" Upon thy glassy watery pall,
" But in these pearly vaults so low,
" Sad earth-born cares thou ne'er shall know,
" In the minowy grottoes of the sea,

" Shall angel-quiet reign with thee;
" Thy marble form so cold and white,
" Shall rest in the shades of oblivious night.
" Sleep on—fair maid, our hollow shell,
".In liquid sounds, bids thee farewell!
" Farewell!—farewell!!"

My Native Land.

There is a radient land of balmy winds,
Of cloudless climes, blue vales, and starry skies,
Where from sweet lips, and lutes low music sighs,
And o'er the pine clad hills the echo dies
Of sparkling stream, that chime through orange bowers,
And tamarind trellis'd vales, where blooming lies
The prairie's wealth of rainbow-tint'd flowers
Fair smiling chil'ren these of genial skies and golden hours.

Land of beauty and country of my soul.
Brave hearts have striven, and true ones died for thee.

Land where the stately pine groves wave
  Where softly glows the sky;
Land of the beautiful and brave,
  Of forests wild and high.

Oh! blest and heav'n-gifted clime,
  Well may thy sons be brave;
Where Freedom's eagle soars sublime—
  Her starry banners wave.

The broad streams here go sweeping by,
  Swift rolling to the sea;

They say as 'twere with a heaving sigh,
"We leave the home of the free."

Thy sunny plains—thy vine-clad hills,
Thy warm and tranquil vales;
Thy sombre woods so dark and still,
Tell spirit-thrilling tales—

Of many a one whose tameless soul,
Sought the deep solitude;
Whose spirit strong and uncontrol'd,
Lov'd independence rude.

Here glides "La Belle Riviere" along,
With softly murmuring tide;
Where many gallant steamers throng,
In majesty and pride.

Along thy brinks sweet natal stream,
How oft I've sought to cast;
Like chaff upon the winds, each dream,
Of all the wildering past.

But no—tho' faded is the flower,
Its fragrance is not done;
So upward come with thrilling power,
Those memories one by one.

And here of old in his bark canoe,
The son of the forest brave;

'Skim'd lightly o'er the waters blue,
  Fleet as the foam-wreath'd wave.

Afar thy cloud-cap'd mountains soar,
  Like a giant warrior band;
Along thy streams—from shore to shore,
  Their brown rocks frowning stand.

How beautiful their blue knobs rise,
  Like ancient battlements they seem;
Bear they no message from the skies—
  A glimpse—a hope—a dream?

Oh! land of heroes, song, and fame!
  May Freedom's eagle fires;
Still warm and wake with kindling flame,
  Our altars and our lyres.

Musings.

Suggested by the untimely death of Thomas Munday, to whose bereaved parents this poem is respectfully inscribed.

Thou art gone home; oh! early crown'd and bless'd
Thou tak'st our summer hence; the flow'r, the tone,
The music of our being all in one,
           .   Depart with thee!—*Mrs. Hemans.*

Thou art passing hence glad summer,
  With all thy wealth of bloom;

And many an earthly treasure,
  Thou bearest to the tomb.

Thou tell'st of home-Elysian,
  Of boundless joys divine;
While on the soul's quick vision,
  Its fadeless summers shine.

Unto our yearning spirit-dreams,
  A deathless thirst thou'st giv'n;
While through thy sun-born glories float,
  Bright imageries of heaven.

Thus list'ning to thy melodies,
  Thy rapt and breezy lay;
Borne on thy rosy pinions,
  Our darling pass'd away.

No more thy breath sweet summer,
  Shall wave his shining hair;
From out those eyes have faded,
  The light that sparkled there.

No more those buoyant footsteps,
  The home-path now shall wend;
Nor with songs of happy children,
  That missing voice shall blend.

Too wildly loved—too early lost,
  Wert thou our household's pride,
But, oh! the gulph that yawns between—
  Dark, fathomless and wide.

If in thy transient wanderings,
    In this our twilight clime;
Among the joy-born blossoms,
    That grace the brinks of Time.

Thou did'st grow weary—tell us;
    Oh! tell, our angel one;
Say was thy soul's brief mission fill'd—
    Thy earthly labor done?

If so, 'twere well indeed with thee,
    Bright heritor of heaven;
No scorpion blight, or grief was thine,
    No sin to be forgiven.

'Tis ours to bear the heavy chain,
    The blight, the sting to know;
While all the heart's deep fountains gush,
    In lava streams of woe.

We call on thee, fair spirit-child,
    Is there in heav'n relief;
For this our bitter sorrow,
    Our dark impotent grief?

Oh! for one smile, sweet spirit,
    One soft responsive tone;
One glance from those lit eyes of joy—
    Our beautiful—our own!

Now softly on night's pinions,
    Low seraph whispers come;

Of hope and joy they're telling,
  In yon bright angel home.

They tell that thou art happy,
  And bid us weep no more;
They tell that we shall meet again,
  Upon that summer shore.

While through the calm air ripples,
  In many a breezy swell;
From light wings gently waving,
  An angel's soft farewell!

———

To ———

"Thou hast aroused within me to a flame
  The embers that had lingered ready to expire;
Thou'st given wings unto my thirst for fame,
  And waked the slumb'ring music of my lyre;
And I would win for thee a deathless name,
  That men should worship and in vain desire."

To thee, god of my lyre, and shrine of holiest thought
I dedicate my verse with in-born music fraught;
To the rich glories of thy mind a tribute pay,
And at thy feet Parnassian garlands lay.
For hast thou not been to me more than friend?
And through the midnight of my soul did'st thou not
  send

To pierce the gloom a pitying ray?
Like starlight o'er a wanderer's way.
Hast thou not made my soul a sacred shrine,
And wakened to a flame its fires divine?
Hast thou not sought the hidden fountains of my
    heart?
And in their depths dost thou not share the angel part?
By the deep sympathies of soul divine,
That made me ever and forever thine;
By the high unities of deathless thought,
By the blest harmonies of heart and mind,
Profound and full—refined and heaven-wrought;
By the strong onenesses that bind,
In sweet according tones the deep heart's lyres;
To thee, forever more, shall thrill my trembling wires,
Within whose tones I'd have thee live when I am cold,
Smit by the Stygean wave sin-born of old,
That 'gainst the many-peopled shores of Time;
Upheaves, where oft we've heard, with deep prophetic
    ear,
Full many a God-awakened spirit chime,
Or billowy sound of life profound and clear.

    *   *   *   *   *

Was it not ours to read—celestially given—
Eternity's text-book, the star written heaven?
And oft in sweet musings and spirit-wrought dreams,
Have we not strayed by those classical streams?
Where the swains of Arcadia awake the soft flute,
In gentle complainings to Love's tender suit;

We have basked in the wealth of fair Thessaly's bowers,
And a chaplet have twined of pale daphne flowers;
A signet of soul—of thought—and of worth,
Sweet boon of the gods to the gifted of earth;
We have dwelt 'neath the shades of Tempe's sweet vales,
And quaff'd the soft breath of Ionian gales;
In the Pyrean fount together we've sought,
A soul-giving draught from its depths to have caught;
We have roamed through the ages of bronze and gold,
And talked with the gods in the temples of old.

Then oh! may the spell, so spiritually given,
Ne'er fade from my heart, or by cold hands be riven.
Oh! light of my life, and light of my soul,
Still point thou the way to some Eden-goal;
Still shine on my heart as a star on the night,
And gild my dark path-way with soul-halos bright;
Like aromas of roses soft floating around,
Thine image shall dwell in my soul's far profound;
And bright be thy day-dreams—while o'er thy repose,
May kind angels gently their white wings close;
Inspire thy wrapt slumbers with visions of light,
Till that last sleep shall fold thee in the bosom of night

Paganini.

It was a beautiful sentiment of the great Italian violinist, that when his mother died, her passing spirit took possession of his violin, inspiring those wizard strains that have charmed the world.

"He touched his harp, and nations heard entranced."—*Pollock.*

Where rolls the Tiber's arrowy tide,
Beneath Italia's rosy skies;
Where in majestic strength and pride,
The purple Appenines arise;
And where the tall Laburnums wave,
And cypress groves and myrtle bowers,
In Tyrrhene deeps their shadows lave;
And spicy winds to fadeless flow'rs,
Expiring songs are whispering;
A potent master minstrel dwelt—
A genius of the silver string,
Whose wildering notes could move and melt,
(As from enchanted chords they flew,)
The stern and cold, the warm and true;
And with a joy intense and new,
Could the enraptur'd soul imbue.
Cradled among the classic rills,
How soft and low, then wild and high,
It burst along the Roman hills,
And warbled in bending sky.
 Not in that gorgeous clime alone,
Those stirring harmonies were heard;
For northern lands had caught the tone

Of thy deep lyre, thou minstrel bird;
In the dark pine groves, and Alpine homes,
And o'er the glacier's icy plains,
Where the bounding chamois hunter roams,
Linger'd those spirit-thrilling strains.
Amidst Ionian isles thy strings
Were heard, their magic sounds prolong d,
In wild, sweet music-murmurings,
So soft, it seem'd those notes belong'd
To some far sphere or spirit-lyre;
So deep the billowy music came—
The breast of flame, the heart of fire,
Those syren songs could soothe and tame.

   And where the surging Baltic foams,
Where dread Black Forest's caverns frown,
Where Albion rears her stately domes—
And Occidental suns go down,
Beyond Atlantic's swelling floods,
On Freedom's eagle-banner'd shore—
Her Indian isles, and grand old woods—
Those melting tones awoke once more.
Where e'er he smote the sounding chords,
Rich, pealing harmonies of song,
Gush'd out among the the wondering hords,
That swept the lofty halls along.
Ripples of sound, then wave on wave,
Of liquid melody arose—
Now ravishing and sweet—then grave,
And full, as gathering water flows;

Again roll'd on those notes profound,
As the hoarse roar of falling floods,
Or battling sounds that shriek around,
In sudden bursts thro' distant woods.
Then dying—falling—soft and low,
As angel voices heard in dreams,
Or evening winds, that gently blow,
O'er dewy vales and silver streams.
Oh! whence those soul-subduing strains;
Born of Apollo's kindling fires?
Decending from celestial plains,
Some seraph o'er the tuneful wires,
Methinks, hath swept its golden wings;
Whence thy power?—enchanter tell?—
Like Passion's dream, that wildly flings
Around the heart its circean spell?
There comes a voice through distant years,
And to my list'ning soul responds,
Like music from the far off spheres,
And through the night of spirit bonds
Draws near—it is the minstrel's own:—
" A mother's voice inspir'd the song,
Her soul's deep voice—her spirit's tone—
As those wild harpings gushed along,
Her spirit free my harp possess'd,
Breathing electric melodies;
Her soul's rich harmonies express'd,
In wild unearthly symphonies.
When weary of the sounds of life,

Her dust sank down to rest at last,
From earthly discord, pain and strife,
And being's fitful dream was past.
Then sweetly from each quivering string,
Her song in many a music-swell,
Would at the touch enchantment bring—
The master's touch—she loved so well."
   The voice is hush'd—the strings are rent—
     Cold is the magic master hand;
   The wizard's mystic power is spent,
     That only could those tones command.

EPITHELAMIUM.

There is a mingling of sweet tones and voices,
Blent with the dewy fragrance of the night;
So wild those strains as when the soul rejoices,
With its o'erflowing fullness of delight,
The old—the young—a happy throng is there,
Bright lamps and dancing feet and garland fair.
      Extract from an unpublished poem.

Away! to the festal halls to-night,
  For youth and beauty will be there;
Upon whose brows the radiance bright,
  Is yet undim'd with care.

Oh! there amid the halcyon bow'rs,
  Is one with eyes of light;
Go twine her hair with orange flow'rs,
  For she will wed to-night.

Emblems of spotless innocence,
  Of purity and truth;
A richer dower than gems of earth,
  She brings that gallant youth.

From her soft eyes no tear-drops fall,
  His brow is free from care;
The doubt that held their hearts in thrall,
  Shall dwell no longer there.

Oh, bliss intense! oh, holy joy!
  When willing hearts and hands
Seal every dear and whispered vow,
  In Hymen's rosy bands.

Then weave of joy, a rosy chain,
  To stay the gorgeous hours;
And o'er each heart let gladness reign,
  These are life's summer flowers.

Lyrics.

Addressed to Theon.—

I bid mine image dwell,
  (Oh! break not thou the spell,)
In the deep wood and by the fountain side.
                    Hemans.

  Straying at noon,
Neath bluest skies of June;

Amid the forest's wealth of summer bloom,
Where every air is heavy with perfume;
While on the breezes rippling round,
Accents of strange sweet wand'ring sound,
    Come whispering by,
    Or gently nigh,
Echo awakes the sound of distant floods,
Through the green dimness of the voiceful woods;
Then oft with thoughts of thee my soul's true friend,
To some still nook my lonely way I wend.
Or when returning from his fiery chase,
  Along the purple fields of space;
    Titan driven,
    His golden car,
  Adown the distant heaven,
    Flashing far;
  Apollo seeks in haste,
    The rosy charms,
Of Occident, whose bosom chaste,
Oft glows with sweet alarms;
    When at her shrine,
    In tones divine;
    Her hunter-king,
  To Love's familiar pleasing,
Wakes the spheres' sweet lute,
Soft as Arcadian shepherd's flute;—
And on the breezy syllables of sound,
Sweet nature's vespers float around.
    Then with the soul,

In sweetest harmony of tone,
    Without control;
    Wand'ring alone,
    O'er balmy meads,
Where showers of summer dew,
Fall down like silver beads;
'Neath which the violets blue,
    Like angels' eyes,
Reflect the dewy radiance of the skies;
    With sad sweet joy,
Shrined in my heart dost thou my secret thoughts employ.
Or when night's stillnesses prevail,
Dim spectral forms in shadows pale,
    Flit through the pleasant gloom;
While soft the locust's bloom,
Upon the night breeze flings,
A breath of painful sweetness,
Like the memory of things,
On the waves of Time departed;
And in their fleetness,
    Sometimes come,
With yearning dreams of home,
And haunt the broken hearted.
Thus oft I think of thee,
My soul's bright sanctuary.
And when the gentle moon,
Throughout night's quiet noon,
Along the Ithureal plain

Doth lead her shining train,
    Of starry sisterhood;
While glittering round a flood,
    Of radient light,
Lays like a robe about the queen of night.
The spirit-flame then more serenely burns;
More fondly then the tender bosom yearns,
    For loved ones gone,
    Or absent friends :—
'Tis then thy spirit's tone,
A sweet enchantment lends,
    To memory's ear,
Profound—and full—and clear.
And oh! how oft, sweet orb,
In childhood's elfin hour,
Thou did'st with mystic power,
My infant mind absorb.
Thus gazing oft on thee,
Thou seem'st a beauteous mystery;
    And I did sometimes deem,
    Thou wert a spirit's dream,—
    Or soul of bright Evangel,—
    Or alien angel,
By powers supernal doomed;
    When Eden fair,
In pristine beauty bloom'd;—
In pale and mute despair,
To wend thy silent way;
With no responsive beam—no self-resembling ray.

Musing alone I sit,
While through the night halls lit,
   With angels' eyes;
   Some spirit sighs,
Upon the perfumed air—
Like some lone string,
In love-tones whispering,
Of joyance deep and visions fair;
Is it thy soul's deep voice,
That bids mine own rejoice?—
Is it thy spirit's ray,
   That from afar;
Bends o'er my twilight way,
A lone and guiding star?—
And will thy soul upon that shore divine,
   Yet know and speak to mine?
   Oh! will these raptures spirit-born,
Illume the soul upon that glorious morn?
   And shall these joys there be complete?
   Or is it but a passing gleam?
      And brief as sweet,—
      A thought—a dream—
      The spirit of a spell,
That in my bosom's infinite must dwell?
   Again I bend mine ear,
   To catch those seraph whispers dear;
While through the still profound,
No murmur wakes around;
Save in the vale remote,

Sad philomelas lonesome note,
    With ceaseless woe,
Floats on Æolean whispers low.
Now comes a dream of tender memories o'er me,
When wrapt in silken bonds of spirit sympathy,
    United oft in by-gone hours,
    'Neath Silvia's pleasant bowers,
    Together we have sought,
    The fane of deathless thought.
      The time is past—
    Those joys are flown;
While on Life's changing surges vast,
Afar from me thy bark floats on—
While like a bird that's on the wing,
'Tis mine in other bowers to sing,
    Or sad or gay,
My gothic roundelay;
But, Theon, when upon thy way,
Thou seek'st some spirit's kindred ray,
Then cast a lingering look behind,
And think of one whose soul and mind,
To thee will like the magnet turn,
And oft with tearful vision yearn,
For that sweet converse of the soul,
Which then was often ours,
    Without control,
In summer evening's pleasant hours;
And may the memory of those days,
Float round thy heart like ruby rays,

Of sundown glories;
And as thy mind oft backward flees,
From present care to some bright spot;
　　Then turn again,
　　To Friendship's fane,
　　Forget it not.

SONGS OF WAR.

No. 1.

THE DEPARTURE.

> All are gone forth—and of that all, how few,
> Perhaps return.   *Sardanapalus.*

There is a radiant land of balmy winds,
Of cloudless climes, mild seas, and starry skies,
Where Pleasure's syrens oft the wand'rer binds,
And from sweet lips, and lutes low music sighs,
And o'er the pine clad hills the echo dies
Of sparkling streams—that came thro' orange bow'rs,
 And tamarind trellis'd vales, where blooming lies
The prairies wealth of rainbow-tinted flowers,
Fair smiling chil'ren these, of genial skies and golden hours.

Hark!—that pealing sound!—'tis the shrill trumpet's
    note,
The forest-hills, and peaceful vales along—
And wild alarums on the rent air float;
War's tocsin rolls—the northern hills prolong
The startling sound—the sword unsheath, be strong—
Our country calls—" To Arms!"—young soldier, rise—
" Away "—thro' hall or bow'r, where Hope's bland
    song
Had whispered Paphean joys, the dread war-cries,
O'er the broad land resounds, and through the bending
    skies.

We saw in pride depart, that battle host;
The good, the brave, the gen'rous and the true;
The old, the young—aye! those we lov'd the most;
We felt their warm hands' clasp, and heard their last
    adieu.
Oh! who can tell if o'er the sad eyes' hue,
Would ever steal the tears of joy at their return?
In dreams we see them yet—their shad'wy forms
    pursue—
Say is it vain for them that our hearts burn—
Will they not heave a sigh, and for their bright homes
    yearn?

Oh! there were partings dread, young cheeks grew
    pale,
And long adieus were told with streaming eyes;
And there were ringing hands, and many a wail—
Low faltering words—and tearful sobs—and sighs,
From woman's heart, with childhood's shrieking cries,
Burst forth.—The low winds rose with gentle swell,
And bore the wail along the tranquil skies,
Till soft and low the mournful cadence fell,
Blending and dying with the sound—Farewell!

SONGS OF WAR.

No. 2.

THE MARCH.

> I knew 'twas a trumpet's note,
> And I see my brethren's lances gleam;
> And their pennons wave by the mountain stream,
> And their plumes to glad winds float.—*Hemans.*

I dwelt in a grand old home, whose sea-girt walls
Rose like some tower of olden time;
Columns of marble strength adorn'd its halls,
While perfum'd light, with music circean chime,
Stole up midst rosy lamps and forms sublime,
Of alabaster mould; and the low sound
Of martial strains, blent with the ocean's hymn;
As on the frowning rocks grey, cold and ivy-crown'd
The wild waves roar'd with fearful bound.

The pale round moon wept down her silver light,
Where slept an army's strength all hush'd and still:
And the sentry lone, with bayonet bright,
Still kept his weary watch—while cold and chill,
The wet dews hung o'er tent and vale and hill,
While far thro' chap'rell groves, the watch-dog bay'd
The wolf;—where wrapt in past or future ill,
By Nuces' falling floods, 'neath the palm-tree's shade,
With folded arms in gloom some lone Camanche stray'd.

Hush'd was the night, and calm the sky-lit bay;
The drill was done—the song, the dance was o'er.

Upon the shad'wy wave in mute array,
The starry host look'd down—and near the shore,
A thousand masts reposed—the flashing oar
No murmurs woke—and loos'd the white sails hung;
While through the dreamy vales and blue seas o'er,
The incense-breathing airs their odors flung—
Oh! fairest land that ever patriot loved, or poet sung.

But hark!—is that the sound of seas I hear?—
Or trump and prancing steed and reveille drum?—
That rous'd from flaming dreams of sword and spear,
The slumbering soldier?—Lo! where in terror dumb,
The foe retires—our arm'd legions come!
With banners proud and streaming pennons white,
And hurried steed—car—mortar and bomb;
While their lances gleam in the rosy light,
Like stars that dance on the glittering seas at night.

Like the phantom forms of a warrior's dream,
In martial pride our wheeling squadrons pass;
O'er scorching plains, wild hills, and rocky streams,
Through tangled beds of cactus green, or dark morass;
There the spotted snake in the tall rank grass,
With deadly fangs in fearful beauty lies.
But where are they—that army vast?—Alas!
The proud hills rise between, e'er the crimson dies
Of early Hesperus fades from eastern skies.

No. 3.

Rio Grande.

The battle gathers like a storm. Soon shall ye hear the roar of death.—Ossian.

Look! where upon the seas the tow'ring masts,
Unfurl'd their banners to the low winds bland,
Where throng'd the shores two armies vast;
And the dark waters of the Rio Grande,
Boom'd thro' the hills, while far along the strand,
In must'ring troops our fierce battalion flew;
Grimly the war-god smil'd—o'er the hot sand,
Dread carnage stalk'd. Ah! there were those who drew,
E'en from their death-pangs, inspiration new.

And there were those whose every thought,
Of grief, or joy, or wish that life inspired;
Or hope sublime, from glory's throbbings caught,
Or deed of good, or ill, or aught the soul desired,
In one dread moment rush'd—and wildly fir'd
The glazing eye.—And there was one who bleeding lay,
Whose thoughts of home in one deep sigh expired;
While by his native streams, unconscious play
His orphan children—and the lone mother kneels to pray—

That *he*, their dying sire, might yet return.
Still from affections cells no tearful lavas gush'd,

Although with seas of grief his dim brain burn'd;
But all at once as from that proud heart, crush'd,
The crimson life-stream flow'd—the moan was hush'd—
The spirit-flame expir'd.—There is a goal
Where the brave triumph, thither hath he rush'd,
Beyond where the dark waters of oblivion roll,
On deathless wings—thence flew the lightning soul.

And moans and shrieks, and curses of despair,
With shouts and savage yells, and piercing cries,
Along the squadrons rent the scorching air,—
And many a glance from dying eyes,
Would seem to say that on their native skies,
They fain would look once more, until afar,
The din of arms, upon his faint ear dies—
While wringing lance—flying steed and rolling car,
Blend with the thunders and the storm of war.

No. 4.

Palo Alto

> As a hundred winds in Lochlin's groves—
> As fire in the pines of a hundred hills—so loud—
> So ruinous—so vast—the ranks of men hewn down.
> Farewell!—thou bravest of men! thou conqueror
> In the field!—But the field shall see thee no more—
> Nor the dark wood be lighted with the splendor
> Of thy steel.—Thou hast left no son.—Future
> Time shall hear of thee—and the song shall
> Preserve thy name.—*Ossian.*

And here o'er Palo Alto's crimson plains,
Now let us pause ;—O ! muse of tragic song—
And o'er the brave—the lov'd—the early slain—
Awake the lyre—in tears the strain prolong.
Who with the brave the lurid field along,
Can fill thy place, O Chief in war ?—Who dare
What ne'er thine eagle eye or spirit strong
Could tame ?—Who cope with thee in battle's glare ?—
Save he, the bold Dragoon of flaming sword and
   streaming hair.

There amid the lightning flash of steel,
And the deep booming of artillery,
Where long and loudest was the deaf'ning peal
Of the dark war-storm and wing'd victories,
On chariot-wheels roll'd through the flashing sea,
Of blood and fiery deaths—a mighty star—
Went out from war's red firmament—he
That fought with the proudest steed and flying car,

The laurel'd Chief, far famed in Seminola's war.

He fell!—But why, or wherefore, who can tell?
Time, the destroyer, in his deathward course,
Yields no reply—but onward sweeps to swell
The gulph of ruin.—Yes, rider and horse
Have fall'n—and bravely, too—without remorse;
For when he felt away the life-drops run,
Nor did his spirit lose its fire or force;
But as he fainting fell, still shouted " on !"
And " on !"—nor reck'd he of the fame he lost or won.

And there, all agonized, was prostrate seen,
Bleeding and spent, his proud war steed,
(The princely gift of Britain's haughty Queen;)
Who once with eye of fire and hoof of speed,
Nor foe—nor flame—nor battle's roar did heed;
But onward rush'd, amid the storm array
Of war, to peril's gaping jaws and war-like deeds,
And foremost fell---biting the earth whereon he lay,
While fast in crimson tides his proud life ebb'd away

Where the dark waters of the Rio Grande,
Respond in music to the sounding shore;
Where fond familiar eyes, or voices bland,
Of those he lov'd shall greet him never more,
The warrior sleeps—and glory's dream is o'er.
Brave Ringgold, fare thee well!—here must we part.
We mourn—but tears will not the dead restore.

Yet nought shall 'rase thy deeds from battle's tragic chart,
Or blot thy memory from a nation's weeping heart.

No. 5.

> * * * * Against some storm,
> We often see a silence in the heavens,
> The bold winds speechless, and the orb below,
> As hush as death.—*Otway.*

There came a pause---and from the flaming field,
Belowna's car retir'd—the ocean rush
Of gathering hosts and steeds had ceas'd---nor peal'd
The deep mouth'd cannon's voice again ;---a hush,
Like that of death, dwelt where the lava gush
Of many lives went out. Oh! strong the chain
That could those proud souls bind, or brave hearts crush.
While music far along the sounding plain
Awakes---and wildly peals in peans o'er the slain.

NOTES TO MEXICAN WAR SONGS.

The foregoing poem was suggested and written at the commencement of the war between the United States and Mexico; but at the fifth number a temporary cessation of hostilities took place, when they were laid aside with the view of being again resumed and concluded, as the circumstances and progress of the war should suggest. Since which period the health of the authoress has been so sadly on the decline, that she abandoned the idea of writing little else than short poems or stanzas, merely to beguile a few invalid hours—hence the abrupt discontinuation of the Mexican War Songs.

Note 1—No. 4, verse 1st.

"Who with the brave the lurid fields along,
Can fill thy place, O Chief in war? &c."

Comparative allusions to Col. May and Maj. Ringgold.

Note 2—No. 4, verse 1st.

"Save he, the bold Dragoon of flaming sword and streaming hair."

Never shall I forget the picture presented to my eye in the stately person of Col. May, mounted on his coal black charger, and, unlike E. P. R. James' solitary horseman, went flying like a phantom over the chaparrell hills, while his wealth of long sunny hair floated like a banner in the wind.

Note 3— No. 4, verse 2d.

"That fought with the proudest steed and flying car,
The laurel'd Chief, far famed in Seminola's war."

Alluding to the victories achieved in the border wars of Florida with the Seminoles.

Note 4—No. 4, verse 4th.

The gallant horsemanship of Maj. Ringgold, and the beauty of his noble steed, elicited my admiration; whereupon I was informed by an officer at my side, that the animal was presented by Queen Victoria to the Major, during his sojourn in Europe. I have never received any further authority on this subject.

Note 5—No 4, verse 5th.

"Where the dark waters of the Rio Grande."

Since the publication of this poem, the remains of this gallant officer have been removed from the Rio Grande to Hagarstown, Maryland.

SONNETS AND SONGS.

Song of the Flowers.

The following fanciful little effusion was suggested to the authoress in a dream.

There's wit in flowers, if we've the wit to gather it.—Shakespear.

 From the morning skies and the sunset's dyes,
  We've borrow'd our blushing hues;
 Here the butter-fly dips its hyblied lips,
  Then its cloud-ward course pursues.

 'Tis the star-rays bright, and the moon's pale light,
  And the burning sun by day;
 The gentle showers in spring-time hours,
  And the dews that vanish away—

 That to us bring, while the free birds sing,
  Our colorings rich and fair;
 From our glowing vases the hum-bird chases,
  The insect tribes of air.

 With rainbow wings the dewlet springs,
  From our emerald leaflets gay;
 And the zephyr's breath, far o'er the heath,
  Our odors beareth away.

Our tinted bowl, is the secret goal,
   Where fairies love to dwell;
Our leaves they fold, and o'er us hold,
   By night, their charmed spell.

Oh! lady fair, we've perfumes rare
   In silence floating on—
Like morning beams, on chiming streams,
   Our lives will soon be gone.

The summer day long, his drowsy song,
   The bumble-bee dreamily hums;
But haste, haste, away, we may not stay,
   When the frosty spirit comes.

Spring.

All Nature joyful, shouts along the plains,
   And echo swells the chorus o'er the hills;
Catch the glad sound, ye music-murmuring rills,
   For Spring in rosy garlands comes again.

How gaily now the Floral Queen,
   In emerald robes assumes her reign;
Blue pansies strewing o'er the plain,
   With daisy wreaths and cowslips green.

On evening's brow her blushes glow,
   Her voice is in the wild bird's song;
And softly floats the streams along,
   Blent with the zephyrs' flute-notes low

Now sporting o'er the dewy lawn,
   Through woody vales and vine-clad bow'rs,
Or thron'd among the May-born flow'rs,
   Her smiles illume the rosy dawn.

Pan's breezy lute among the whisp'ring reeds,
Awakes the Nymphs with many a sylvan call;
From grottoes dark, where silvery fountains fall,
While fairies dance along the moon-lit meads.

To a Friend.

When the dusky shades of night,
   With noiseless steps are creeping;
And Luna's silver light,
   On vale and hill is sleeping
I'll hie me then away,
   To my lonely wood-land bow'r,
Beneath the shadows gray,
   Of twilight's sombre hour.

O! wilt thou come with me?
   When chiming streams are bringing;
A dream-like minstrelsy,
   In sylvan echoes ringing;
When soft decending dews,
   Be-gem each queenly flower,
And swift the night-bird 'sues
   The glow-worm to his bower?

Say does thy sensate heart,
   O'erflow with ardent feeling?
Dost feel the tear-drop start,
   When holy thoughts come stealing?
Thou'lt love the mystic hour,
   And drink its softness in,
Thy soul will feel its pow'r,
   And know its calm within.

When down the woody dell,
   The summer winds are straying;
When day hath bid farewell,
   And light the stars are raying—
Come then with steps so light,
   With that true heart of thine,
And eyes so like the night
   As darkly bright they shine.

Then will some fairy sprite
   With evening shades descending,
Glide round in haloes bright,

Each thought and feeling blending;
Come seraph of my dreams—
Star of my lonely soul;
Come with thine eyes bright beams,
And lend thy lov'd control.

STANZAS.

To a Class-mate.

We met when the first gush of youth,
   Was beating free, and hopes were high;
Our lips breath'd nought but tales of truth,
   And our young bosoms heaved no sigh.

In rainbow glories, pure and bright,
   To us did all things seem to gleam;
Thy smiles were bland, thy steps were light,
   No grief disturbed thy halcyon dream.

At dewy twilight's elfin hour,
   How oft I've wander'd forth with thee;
And felt the spirit-soothing pow'r,
   Of gentle friendship's sympathy.

There oft enchanting music's swell,
   We've heard amid the odorous gale;

With " wood notes wild " from flow'ring dell,
   And streams that chime along the vale.

Ah! still that joy-dream of the past,
   Around my riven heart shall twine;
Like a green spot on mem'ry's waste,
   Or ivy round the broken shrine.

Or like the breath of faded flowers,
   That lingers round the snowy urn;
Back to my heart those sinless hours,
   On memory's wings return.

ISABELL.

The following "Petite" effusion was suggested to the authoress on becoming acquainted with a very interesting little girl, who was exceedingly precocious for her years.

Oh! who hath seen my Isabell?—
Her witching ways 'twere hard to tell,
Her sylph-like form and angel grace,
Her lightsome step, and smiling face,
These are the charms that ever dwell,
Around my little Isabell.

The neck of snow and eyes of blue,
Her cheek a rose-bud bursting through,
The sunny brow and auburn curls,

The ruby lips and teeth of pearls,
Charms which my heart remembers well,
Of beauteous little Isabell.

Her smile like morning's rosy light,
Illumes my sadden'd heart to-night,
Her merry song now sweetly trills,
Like bird-notes ringing o'er the hills,
Or flute-note echoes in the dell—
The syren voice of Isabell.

Pure is her heart as mountain snows
Where deep the fount of kindness flows,
And gentle in her mirthfulness,
As is an angel's soft caress,
Ah! these are charms my bosom swell,
For charming little Isabell.

Oh, should you meet this little fair,
Your heart she surely would ensnar
An houri strayed from Eden's grove
Or wand'ring star-beam from above,
Mission'd awhile with us to dwell,
Is joyous little Isabell.

Written in a Lady's Album.

They tell me thou art young,
Then I will guess thee fair,
And like the wings of midnight,
Thy softly flowing hair;
Bright as a summer sea,
Reflecting bluest skies,
The smiling witchery,
That floats within thine eyes.

I ween there's many a charm,
And many a nameless grace,
Adorns thy gentle form,
And lights thy rosy face;
And better far thy heart,
All glad and fancy free,
Around thee doth impart,
A joy-born melody.

Thus ever glad and free,
May Virtue's ægis bright,
Lay like a robe about thee,
And shield thy heart from blight,
And soft as evening winds,
That sigh o'er summer streams,
Be every link that binds,
Thy heart to rosy dreams.

To a Portrait.

Say, Portrait! whence the pleasing spell,
   That binds me to this place;—
Why does my heart with rapture swell
   While gazing on thy face?

Enchanter! sovereign of my soul,
   I'd here forever stray;
Here silent weep without control,
   And sigh myself away.

Oh! might I round those breathing charms,
   In sinless purity;
Enraptured wreathe my clasping arms,
   Unknown to even thee.

The Pagan priest adores the sun,—
   The Heathen gods of clay;
But dearest semblance thou hast grown,
   More idolized than they.

To ———

Sweet Friend! it was a rosy hour,
   The festive time when first we met;
Midst mirth and song whose circean power,
   Forbids that I should e'er forget.

How oft I've sought some sylvan bower,
  To wake the harp of memory;
Recalling oft the palmy hour,
  When first I learned to think of thee.

And when the gentle evening star,
  Looks down in love on thee and me;
Then in my western home afar,
  I watch that star and think of thee.

When sorrow darkened o'er my way,
  And wrapt my soul in misery:
Thy name hath lent a pitying ray,
  To pierce the gloom with thoughts of thee

What though upon my throbbing heart,
  Death's icy chains should fastened be;
What though the light of life depart,
  My latest thought shall be of thee.

And yet those palmy bowers of light,
  While thou wert slumb'ring quietly,
I'd leave;—and through the jewel'd night,
  A guardian spirit prove to thee.

Stanzas.

Oh! wake once more that mournful strain,
    Around me fling its haunting spell;
Oh! let me hear those sounds again,
    Of joy-dreams past their accents tell

Yes; touch again the trembling string,
    What scenes those mournful sounds recall;
While memories dark, their shadows fling,
    Upon the past a sombre pall.

When first I heard that music's swell,
    I stood within the spacious hall;
The light in streamy glories fell,
    Along the lofty parien wall.

And there were dazzling forms and bright,
    The proud, the beautiful were there;
My young heart trembled with delight,
    And fluttered with a secret snare.

For there was one who watched my step,
    And by me ever lingered nigh;
On me his ardent gaze still kept,
    And softly breathed a languid sigh.

The scene is past and faded quite,
    The image fled and my heart's rest;

Yet many a vision of that night,
　　On memory's tablets are impressed.

Oh! that this heart which now is breaking,
　　In Lethe's stream might ever sleep;
For fell despair my soul is shaking,
　　And hopeless I am doomed to weep.

Hush! hush! my soul, the music's ended,
　　Yet let me hear one gush again;
There's grief and joy so sweetly blended,
　　I could expire upon that strain.

Song.

In sadness I languish for thee love,
　　For thee I impatiently call;
O! come to our old willow tree love,
　　Where murmuring waters fall.
O come! O come! O come! dearest beloved come

The whippowil sings of her mate love,
　　From yonder lone beachen tree;
Thus lonely thy presence I wait love,
　　Thus lonely I sing of thee.
O come! O come! O come! dearest beloved come

Soft zephyrs are sighing low love,
    Adown our own sweet vale;
Where oft we have wandered slow love,
    And breathed the ambrosial gale.
O come! O come! O come! dearest beloved come!

I go, but by yonder star love,
    That beams on thee and me;
Although I may wander afar love,
    Yet fondly I'll still think of thee.
Farewell! farewell! farewell! dearest beloved farewell!

STANZA.

Oh! ye dreary days of sadness,
    Clothed in funeral array;
Days of youthful joy and gladness,
    Now forever pass'd away.

Mine was once the heart of gladness,
    Pleasure's cup I gaily sip'd;
'Tis broken now—and grief and madness,
    With bitter dregs now bathe my lips.

What to me is beauteous nature,
    Faded are the charms of spring;
Lost to me her loveliest feature,
    No joy to me the seasons bring.

Even music's notes of sweetness,
    Has sorrow in its floating song;
Of by-gone days and of their fleetness,
    It whispers as it floats along.

Cease, warbling lyre, my heart is breaking,
    Nay, tell to me that tale no more;
Despair is from her trance awaking,
    And every dream of hope is o'er.

FANTASIES.

The breezes all met in a bower one day,
To frolic the noon-tide hours away.
"Hush! soft! be still!"—young Zephyrs said,
"On this bed of flowers reposes a maid,
I'll softly fan the brow of the girl,
Then nestle me in some clustering curl."
And thus around her a watch they kept,
Inspiring her dreams as soft she slept.
Escaped from her eyelids' silken fringe
Stood a tear, bedewing her cheeks soft tinge.
One kiss'd the pearly gem away,
When a butterfly came of pinions gay;
"Begone!" they cried—"you will break her repose,
Her cheek you have rudely mistook for a rose,"
And that thieving bee now reveling sips,

The nectar from off her balmy lips.
" Fly away noisy bee—we are sorely afraid,
With your humming and buzzing you'll wake the maid."
Then in glee their pinions sweet they spread,
And from them a thousand odors shed ;
One swept her lute's soft trembling strings,
Another kept time with his sportive wings,
And gaily flut'ring one gentle wind,
Breathed a much loved name to her dreaming mind.
She murmur'd low and sighed the name,
And whispered of a secret flame.
The laughing breezes heard the maid,
And flew round in a whirl as thus they said,
" Make haste and scour the sunny plain,
And bear it to the favored swain."
Alarmed the maid awaken'd sigh'd,
" Yield back that name." " Nay," Zephyrs cried,
And he wrapt it in his frolic wing,
" I'm off," said he, " in a twinkling."
So saying, away the babbler flew.
" Ye reckless swains, to which of you
Was told the tale ? If I only knew
'Twas the right one. What then ? Confess it true ?
Well, really—I—I'll be—blam'd if I do."

Response to ——

"Alas! what grief should thy heart know?"

'Tis not by outward sign or show,
The deep heart's anguish we can know;
We cannot fathom Passion's storm,
By writhing brow or faded form;
Or in the tearful torrent's start,
That lava fountain of the heart,
What tho' the brow seem free from care,
The lips be wreathed in smiles all fair;
Within the brain a pool of fire,
May rage and burn and not expire;
And on the heart a curse may lie,
That still consumes yet will not die.
What tho' the step be light as air,
The heart may burn with rankling care,
And writhe and break in mute despair.

To Miss Amanda Harte.

I have never known thee, never met thee,
Yet is my roving fancy prone to set thee
Like a fair picture in my mental vision,
Born half of earth and half of realms Elysian.

All heart I ween thou art by name and nature :
A warm, confiding, young and joyous creature ;
And like the *hart* that nimbly thro' the wild-wood,
Seeks the green dell where falls the fountain flood,
Be thy heart free and clothed with innocence,
Serene and pure as the bright stars from whence
Youth's happiest hopes and vision-dreams are caught,
And may thy future lot with heaven-hues be fraught.

Song.

Around another's brow,
    The myrtle wreath I'll twine ;
Thou dost not love me now,
    I am no longer thine.

Before another's shrine,
    Thou'st bent the suppliant knee ;
Thou call'st her divine—
    Thou said'st the same of me.

Thine ever changing heart
    Upon the altar lay ;
Its fires will soon depart,
    Its incense pass away.

Thine image on my heart,
    I now no longer wear ;

I do not grieve to part,
  My brow is free from care.

The illusion now is o'er,
  I do not think of thee;
I dream of thee no more,
  Of what thou wast to me.

Low hov'ring round my head,
  Ethereal visions play;
And softly from my bed,
  Charm all sad dreams away.

The shadows of the past
  Like night have fled away;
While Love around me casts,
  Its bland and ardent ray.

Thou'lt meet me in the throng,
  Again will see me smile;
Wilt press my careless hand,
  Nor cause one thrill the while.

Around another's brow,
  The myrtle wreath I'll twine;
Thou may'st not love me now,
  Since I'm no longer thine.

To Mary Bell.

Sweet Mary Bell—that gentle name,
    Is linked with many a spell;
My aching breast has felt no rest,
    Since thee I met, sweet "Mary Bell!"

Her gentle voice sank in my heart,
    As low its accents fell;
I strove to speak—my voice grew weak,
    I only sigh'd—sweet "Mary Bell."

Her sylph-like form and witching face,
    Where all the Loves doth dwell;
The silken lash whence glances flash,
    Hath won my heart, sweet "Mary Bell."

As oft on me her glances fall,
    Soft as a young gazelle's;
A thrilling flame darts through my frame,
    I feel I love thee—"Mary Bell."

But hush! my weak and faltering tongue
    Can ne'er my feelings tell;
Oh! is it vain, the tender pain,
    I endure for "Mary Bell?"

Song.

The circean spell is over,
    The Paphean dream is done;
The mystic cord is broken,
    That bound our hearts in one.

And gentle Love lies weeping,
    Above the urn of Hope;
The flowers of mem'ry keeping
    To guild Life's downward slope.

The last fond word is spoken,
    The murmur'd prayer is o'er;
The spirit-lute is broken,
    'Twill sound in song no more.

A Dream of the Past.

*"Thy voice is in mine ear, sweet friend;
Thy look is in my heart."*

I'm thinking now of one,
    Beloved in distant years;
And fondly cherish'd still,
    Through pain and bitter tears.

That one to me how dear,
    No tongue can ever tell;
How deep within my heart,
    The haunting dream must dwell.

I see thee even now,
    And as when last we met;
My breaking heart is full,
    Mine eyes with tears are wet.

They're floating in my mind,
    The look—the smile—the tone—
The tender kiss of love,
    Which once were all mine own.

The light of all my life,
    And life of every dream;
As soft Hesperus shines,
    On some benighted stream.

Oh! for one gentle glance,
    From those Ithureal eyes;
One tone of that sweet voice,
    As soft as summer sighs.

Or might I clasp once more,
    The hand that once was mine;
And greet that pleasant smile,
    As angels look divine.

What were a world of joy,
    To exstacies like these;

Or richest argosies,
  That float upon the seas?

Within my soul's profound,
  There is a sacred spot;
Serenely calm, and where
  The world's breath enters not

Oh! there for aye, enshrined,
  A gentle form is set;
And ne'er till life is o'er,
  Shall I that dream forget.

THE SERENADE.

I leaned me on the midnight air,
  The wind was sighing low;
The youthful moon adown the West,
  Hung like a silver bow.

Methought if I were but a ray,
  How softly I would shine
Into thine eyes, and silently
  Read every thought of thine.

When soft a manly voice arose,
  How deep and rich its tone;

My pulses paused—my heart grew still
  I heard but that alone.

Entranced I heard the witching song,
  As oft it rose and fell;
And memory still those sounds prolong,
  As with a magic spell.

Ah! sing again, who e'er thou art,
  I'll listen tho' it kill;
Within the chambers of my heart,
  Those sounds are echoing still.

Song.

Thou didst lure me from the circle,
  Of the cherished and the true;
Midst streams and hills and woodlands,
  Alone to dwell with you.

But the joyous dream is fleeting,
  As fast the moments roll;
It is our last wild meeting,
  To mingle soul with soul.

In sorrow I must wander,
  O'er scenes that's fair no more;

And oft my heart will ponder,
  On blissful hours o'er.

Fare thee well! farewell forever!
  Since we, alas! must part;
'Twere hard indeed to sever,
  'Twill break—'twill break my heart.

When the moon's pale beam reposes,
  Along the quiet sea;
Then in thy bower of roses,
  Oh! dearest, think of me.

ÆOLIAN MELODIES.

Where of ye, O Tempests, is the goal?
Are ye like those that shake the human breast,
Or do ye find, like eagles, some high nest?—Byron.

The winds, the loud high winds, whose mournful choir
Of many voice blent, sends forth their varied notes,
From the hoarse roaring of assembled floods,
To the low whispers breathed to trembling flowers,
As they upon soft summer's lap expire;
Oh! these, from sinless childhood's rosy dawn,
Have a strange spell upon my spirit flung—
While floating round my brain, were shad'wy thoughts
Of dream-like beauty, as my spirit oft
Caught the strange meaning of their anthems wild.
Are they not messengers divine, whose songs,
Eternal, are forever fraught with sounds,
Caught from celestial spheres? And then again,
So near the earth they seem to bend their wings,
That their glad strains are blent with wailing tones
Of mortal cares.
       And oft in mine imagings,
I've heard commingling with their shrieking songs,
Voices, which rose from earth in sad lament,
For those — the lov'd — the good — the brave — the
    pure—

The beautiful and true—too early lost!
When o'er fair Nature's cheek stern autumn casts
The fitful hectic of decay, I've heard,
As wand'ring through the vistas blue,
Of woodlands beautiful, this minstrel band
Come moaning up the vales, and wildly breathe
Their dirge-like melodies.

   'Tis then my soul,
With sweet intelligences rapt, communion sweet—
Communion most divine—doth seem to hold;
And to shuffle off this mortal coil I long,
Of all its earthly film, to have my vision cleared;
To feel my soul expand its unknown powers:
Its wings stretch forth, and far beyond these fields
Of azure soar, where, in the bless'd abodes,
Of etherializing joys I might forever dwell.
But hark! e'en now amid the giant boughs
Of yonder towering woods, in war-like strife,
Their trumpet blasts I hear—and sorrowing tales,
To those of exiled spirits lost akin,
Unto my rapt and list'ning ears are borne.

The Exile's Lament.

 They bear me hence, my native land,
  Far, far away from thee;
 From loving friends—a kindred band—

On o'er the surging sea.
They bear me hence o'er foaming deeps,
   To that benighted shore ;
Where many a weary exile sleeps,
   To wake and weep no more.

They waft me from thy happy scenes,
   Thy merry dancing rills ;
Thy waving woods and vales serene,
   And heaven-soaring hills ;
While from the dark pines waving high,
   With deep and solemn swell,
Are wafted on the wind's low sigh,
   Sad murmurs of farewell.

Now lowly cot, and vaulted dome,
   Are fading fast from view ;
And thou, alas! my boyhood's home,
   Must vanish with them too.
Yet will the glory of your skies,
   Your ever flashing streams,
And many a glance from loving eyes,
   Still haunt my fever-dreams.

Ah! now they're gone—they're shut from sight,
   Behind the ocean wave ;
Oh! for one glance, those visions bright,
   In memory's glass to save ;
Where is the wrong ?—may I not know ?—
   Ye men of power, tell why,

To alien climes why doom'd to go—
  In gloom to toil and die?

Cease—cease, my bursting heart give o'er,
  Since exile chains are thine;
Once more adieu, my native shore,
  Britannia, home of mine.
*   *   *   *   *   *
Like flute notes sweet the waving whispers glide,
Then swelling on, so mournful and yet wild,
That its deep tones still float within my heart.
*   *   *   *   *   *
But hark! there is a gush of melody,
Strange and sweet, as when the summer winds, low
And tremulous, over rich harp-strings sweep;
And on those chaunting cadences of sound, methinks
Some sorrowing spirit's voice in haunting tones is borne.

The Broken Hearted.

The moon is forth, the stars are bright,
The earth is passing fair to-night,
But still mine eyes with tears are wet,
For one whom I can ne'er forget;
Who round my brows once loved to twine,
The pale white rose and myrtle vine;
Oh! he is gone—and joy has flown,
My broken heart has lost its tone,

And burning tears and wasting care,
Have chased the smiles I used to wear.

Alone I roam o'er hill and dell,
To cull the flowers he lov'd so well,
And by the shadowy lake I stray,
Where oft we met at close of day.
Ah! there I've vainly hoped to see,
My once fond lover come to me.
Oh! have I loved him all too well?
Let my woe and anguish tell;
By all that yields me no relief,
By my sleepless nights of grief,
By my brain's wild misery,
I have worship'd faithfully,
With the soul's most mad'ning thrill,
And as madly worship still.

Tell me, ye winds, ye spheres divine,
If aught ye know of lover mine?
Tell me, ye viewless sprites of air,
Is he false to me—the young and fair?
At another's shrine doth Theon dare
To breathe the same impassioned prayer,
That was his wont in happier hour
To breathe within this rose-wreath'd bow'r?
And doth he for that maiden's sake,
His charmed mandolin awake?
Or sleeps he 'neath the ocean wave,
In a pearl-spared cell of the sea maid's cave?

(F)

Or battling 'mid the stern and brave,
Hath my hero found a glorious grave?

I have mourned my life away,
And the hectic of decay,
O'er my cheek and o'er my brow,
Burns intensely even now.
I have sighed and wailed for him,
Till life and all its joys look dim;
But the wasted, broken heart,
May suffer on—endure the smart;
And so intense may be its woe,
That its tears will cease to flow:
The brain may burn with Passion's fire,
The spirit break, and not expire.

Wrapt in shadows pale and dim,
Where I shall not dream of him,
I soon shall know death's placid sleep,
And o'er me roses pale shall weep.
Oh! parent earth, upon thy breast,
Take thy woe-worn child to rest.
* * * * * *
The lute-like winds now faintly fall,
And down the distant glades in sorrowing tones expire.
* * * * * *
But hark! again those melancholy sounds,
Like plaintive voices on the sobbing winds arise,
And as they fall upon my listening ear
Methinks their tones from dying innocence were caught,

As o'er its lowly couch soft zephyrs sighed,
And with the chime of many mingling sounds,
With odors, dew, and summer flowers were blent,
And gently wafted on. Tell us, ye winds,
Do we not hear upon your murmurs borne,
Some deathless spirit's voice, whose yearning car
Hath drank the music of angelic choirs?

The Dying Boy.

Mother! where am I?—and what ails me now?
Oh! I'm so weary—and—I cannot rest;
For some strong hand is pressing on my breast,
The damps of death are settling on my brow.

I scarce can hear your voice—your face looks dim—
Oh! mother shall I ne'er behold thee more?
Hark! nearer they come, from heaven's celestial shore,
Those voices soft of harping seraphim.

Oh! mother, shall I ne'er go forth with thee,
O'er the sweet fields and by the sparkling streams?
Shall none of all my boyhood's glory dreams
Be here fulfilled? Oh, speak to me!

And shall I ne'er behold the morning sun,
Or watch the mountain clouds that chase along the sky;
Or the pale moon that beams at noon of night on high,
Or count the stars when the bright day is done?

No, mother, no; for from beyond yon brilliant dome,
Methinks some heavenly seraph now is hov'ring near;
And this sweet summon falls upon mine ear:
Sweet brother mine, come to the skies with me,
                              Come home.

And now I feel death's icy surges round me swell.
Oh, mother! mother! weep not when I'm gone;
For we shall meet again upon that other dawn;
Then wipe away your tears—'twill not be long—
    farewell!
    *   *   *   *   *   *
Like Memnon's sweet uncertain sun-awaken'd strains,
Those plaintive murmurs died away.
More sadly still the grieving zephyrs sigh,
As tho' upon the sorrow-laden air
A fearful change had pass'd; its fitful moan,
Along the purple hills and twilight vales,
In sobbing accents falls, so mournful and yet wild,
As tho' the heart with anguish full would break.

The Mother's Lament.

Alas! my only hope of this cold gloomy earth,
Last link of life—my dream—my pride—my joy—
Thou wert to me, my gentle, darling boy;
But now thou art gone, leaving desolate my hearth.

Gone—gone, indeed!—and yet how sadly sweet
Death's stillness, like a robe, lays gently round thee

That I could almost dream thou didst but sleep,
And soon again would wake thy mother's smile to
    greet.

How sweet the smile thy pleasant eyes could give;
And oh! how oft these locks of sunny hair
I've parted from thy brow, so ivory white and fair,
While in thy gentle voice my very soul did live.

As some rude child with untaught sway,
O'er a voluptuous harp oft idly flings
His uncouth hands across its strings,
Sundering chords attuned to sweetest lay—

So death, with blackened wings,
Hath swept his icy fingers o'er thy heart;
Where gushing sweet did living harmonies upstart,
And severed all its thousand strings.

The cup is full—the music of my life is hushed—
Come soon, O death, and grant thy Lethean sleep;
There is no grandeur here for thee to reap,
My being's light is gone—my heart is crushed.
   *   *   *   *   *   *
Died on the summer air the melting strain,
And as the sighing gales flew softly by,
They seemed to nestle in the tall rank grass,
And fold their dewy wings.
                      And yet again,
Those gentle airs in whispers low did breathe

Unto the trembling flowers of earth-born cares,
Who bent their weeping heads and quivering leaves,
And sighed their tender perfumes on the night.

The Orphans.

Why, brother, is thy brave young brow,
    Where soft the dark locks lay,
All shaded o'er with sorrow now,
    When all the world looks gay?

Oh! ask me not, my sister dear,
    Too young and fair thou art,
To know what brings the swelling tear,
    The anguish of my heart.

For we are orphans now, alone,
    From place to place must roam;
Our parents, once so kind, are gone,
    We have no friends or home.

Where stands embower'd on the hill
A cottage white, around whose walls
The creeping woodbine twines, and still
The gay glad streamlet falls.

There, once in happiness we dwelt,
    And oft the altar round,
In prayerful breathings lowly knelt,
    While peace our labors crowned.

But change came o'er the scene of bliss,
    And draped our hearts in gloom;
Then came the misery of this,
    Our dark and early doom.

In freedom's wars our father died,
    Upon a distant shore;
Fain would I slumber by his side,
    To wake and weep no more.

Then o'er each heart and brow there came
    Dark clouds of doubt and fear;
We were too sad to breathe his name,
    He was to us so dear.

For strangers cold our home we left,
    In grief and want to dwell;
Each heart grew sick—of hope bereft,
    And sighed to home—Farewell!

At length our gentle mother died,
    Who used to love us so.
No friend have we—no home—Ah! me:
    Oh, who'll protect us now!

    *   *   *   *   *   *

In low complainings ceased those wind-waked strains,
But now my solemn ear drinks in a wail of woe,
So sad, 'twould seem the very winds did weep.

The Bereaved.

Oh, heavily the hours glide,
For she who erst dwelt by my side,
Is now no more—my gentle bride,
           Lost, lost Iannie!

Her tender eyes were like the hue,
Of modest voilets shining through
A tissuey veil of pearly dew—
           Lovely Iannie!

Soft on her brow the silken hair,
Lay goldenly in tresses fair;
Her cheek was like the rose-bud rare—
           Beautiful Iannie!

Joyous and happy as a child,
Would she sing so sweetly wild:
Oh, she was gay and yet so mild,
           Gentle Iannie!

But now my dreams of joy are o'er;
The star hath set that I adore;
Its beams will glad my soul no more—
           Lost, lost Iannie!

I have loved the wildly well;
O, what can my heart's anguish quell?
'Tis nought but death! Till then—Farewell,
           Sweet, sweet Iannie!

*   *   *   *   *   *

Distant, in sobbing tones, the viewless winds,
Amid the dark green pines, arise and softly sigh
In syllables of breezy sound—Farewell!
But now, like angry floods, harsh tones awake,
And fiercely roar along the bending sky.
  * * * * * *

The Captive Chief.

Long years in these prison walls I have pined,
 With the tyrant's chain over me ever;
And long have I struggled the chain to unbind,
 This thraldom dark to sever.
Alas! 'twill be my only tomb,
Companioned for age by silence and gloom.

They may bind these limbs with burning chains;
 They may rack this writhing frame:
But they never can conquer with torturing pains,
 A fearless spirit of flame.
They cannot subdue the chainless mind,
Nor the freeborn soul with fetters bind.

Curse on, curse on, ye minions of power;
 Bring fire, bring faggot—I reck not my fate;
Nor lament I in sadness the soul-mad'ning hour,
 That ye bound me in chains, and thus taught me to hate.
My spirit is free in these prison walls,
As the sky-soaring bird in its forest-halls.

And proud as the eagle that swoops o'er the hills,
Is my tameless soul and its fetterless will;
Your mercy I spurn, and your tortures defy,
And sooner than yield I gladly would die.

Aye, whate'er betide, I ne'er will give o'er;
  For the soul that can triumph o'er death and its foes,
Fair Freedom shall weep when I am no more,
  And love, though afar, shed a tear to my woes.

* * * * * *

Now swelling on, one piercing shriek it gives,
And on swift pinions takes its flight through space
Dying in echoes low amid the trees.

* * * * * *

With transing spell some viewless sprite now sweeps
Its breezy lyre, and soft æolian warblings wake,
While on the dreamy murmurs come sweet strains
Of long ago, and memories of home.

The Captive Exile.

Oh sad was my fate when in youth's sweet prime,
  From my vine-clad home I strayed,
Alone to roam in a foreign clime,
  Where fate my footsteps staid.
In dreams I wander back again,
  To childhood's joyous hour,
To friends and home—the heart's sweet fane,
  Beyond oppression's power.

ÆOLIAN MELODIES. 171

How oft have I loved in my mountain streams,
    'Neath the forest shades to lave;
Where the glory of boyhood's elfin dreams
    Went floating on the wave;
And glad through the aisles of the voiceful woods,
    Resounded the hunter's horn;
Where swift o'er twilight fell and flood,
    The light fawn skip'd at morn.

The herds I see from the dim blue hills,
    Wend o'er the distant plain;
The dark-eyed maid her rude lay trills—
    My heart drinks in the strain;
Sweet haunting memories arise,
    And float around my soul,
Of voices dear and radiant eyes,
    And home the young heart's goal.

    *   *   *   *   *   *

A fearful change shrieks on the yelling blast.

    *   *   *   *   *   *

'Tis vain—'tis vain—o'er my cheek and brow.
    Grief's plague spot, like a cankering fire,
Intensely burns. My sad soul now
    Knows only one desire;
A boon that death alone can give—
    One draught from Lethe's midnight wave
Oh! dying heart, how long canst thou thus live!
    Answer O Death! O Grave!

I have spent my life in these prison walls,
  With a bursting heart and a brain of fire;
And I've sadly wept for my father's halls,
  Till it seemed that my life would expire.
The dream is past, its hues have fled;
  The heart-wish now departed:
For hope is crushed and joy is dead,
  And I am broken-hearted.

I hear at last the death trump call;
  My soul shall have its meed;
And from my limbs the chains shall fall—
  These prison walls recede.
The music of celestial wings,
  In breezy murmurs low,
Unto my heart a joyance brings,
  Like strains of long ago.

Mine eyes wax dim, and faint mine ear;
  Life's earth-born sounds depart;
Death's pulseless hand, with grasp severe,
  Is laid upon my heart.
Yield, yield—O, dying heart give o'er;
  Of joys superne these raptures tell—
O poor crushed heart—forever more.
  The spirit weeps to thee, Farewell.
   *   *   *   *   *   *
The wail hath ceased, and on the voiceless air mute
  silence reigns.

* * * * * * *
   List, list—in hollow moans,
Its own wild requiem of solemn plaints,
The grieving spirit breathes, all fraught with **sad**
  unrest,
And inborn woe.

Euthanasia.

Oh, were it not better far to die,
And in the Lethean tomb to lie;
Than thus to live and tortured be,
In burning chains of misery?
There's nought in life for me to quaff,
But pain and woe—a bitter draught.
Joy sends no sweetened chalice here,
No sunshine on my path to cheer
The wand'rer o'er life's dreary wild;
Nor gleam of hope with radiance mild,
To chase the glooms that o'er my way,
Shuts out the light of life and day.
No tone from life's great lyre around,
Falls on mine ear—a pleasant sound;
No soul akin or answering tone
Responds unto my spirit's moan;
No hue of bliss, except in dreams,
That sometimes o'er my slumber gleams,
As shines the pale sweet wand'ring light
Of Cynthia thro' the clouds of night—

Too sweet to last, too bright to rest,
Like vermil fading from the West;
And joy and hope, and glory's beams,
Are but the light of passing dreams—
Shadows of some supernal clime,
When God shall close the Book of Time,
And open on our yearning sight,
A volume of seraphic light.
Then, at his word the soul shall soar
Through bright infinitudes of lore—
Eternity's broad page explore,
And quaff its truths and thirst no more.

Oh, could I sleep the sleep of death,
I'd gladly yield my struggling breath.
Could I but find that dreamless rest—
That long deep slumber of the blest:
For they are blest who die at last,
Shut out from life's dread battle blast,
And sink to that serene repose,
O'er which the sable wings shall close,
Of death and night, forever more.
Would I might leave Time's dreary shore,
And find oblivion of the soul,
Where cold the Stygian surges roll—
Death's solemn folds across my breast
I'd gently wrap, and seek my rest.
Grant me, ye fates, this last behest:
Let me but sleep, and I am blest.

* * * * * *
Away, like ocean's swelling surges, died,
On distant hills, those sad Euterpean strains.
* * * * * *
And now, methinks, deep organ-tones I hear,
Borne on the stately winds, sad, solemn, and
sublime.

Sorrows of Genius.

Long years I have toiled in the mines of thought,
With a yearning soul and a brain o'er-wrought;
I have shut myself out from the haunts of men—
From Fashion's mart and Deception's fen;
From the festive board and the halls of mirth—
The social throng, round the cheerful hearth;
From the youthful band, who with twinkling feet,
In the gay, glad measures of joyance meet,
Where the syrens of love in their sweet bow'rs sing,
And over young hearts their soft spells fling.
Aye, the things of all time, for this lonely cell
I have left, with my thoughts and my soul to dwell;
Till with heart-sick'ning woe and with sorrow of mind
For some kindred tone, my lonesome soul pined;
Till mine eyes waxed dim and my cheeks grew pale,
And the heaven-borrowed hues of earth did fail;
Thro' blight, and thro' pains, and thro' struggling tears,
It hath lain on my heart and burnt for years;
This deep mountain thirst for God-given truth,

For all science and lore ; till the fires of youth,
And its vigor of thought are extinguished and dead—
Till hope hath departed and Love's light hath fled ;
In multitudes mixed my soul stands alone,
Now distanced from men, by the mind's wave upborne ;
In the great harp of being there's no answering tone—
There's nothing in life to love or to mourn.
I have worshiped wildly in Learning's fane—
Through blood and through fire, through anguish and pain ;
And thus I had madly hoped to have caught
The undying hues of God-gifted thought ;
Some heart-breathing tone from Apollo's rapt lyre,
Or soul-waking spark of Promethean fire,
That should mount o'er the storms and the ruins of time,
Like a star on the night, immortal, sublime.
But, where is the wealth in the temple of lore,
The glittering thought-gems the brain had in store ;
The spoils of the mind, and the deep soul-strain ?
Are they gone with the dreams that return not again ?
Oh, what can assuage the deep thirst of my soul ?
The race is not won, and unreached the goal ;
For the grasp of the mind stops not with the stars,
But still soaring on till eternity bars
The soul's deathless fount, and the source of all light
From the spirit's deep thirst and its yearning sight.
Oh, a fearful boon to my soul was given !

Too brightly tinged—too much of heaven,
Are my life's burning dreams, and too strong the chain
That around my deep heart-affection hath lain.
The web of my being's too etherially wrought—
Too heaven-born the music my soul's ear hath caught;
For the raptures of earth too spiritually given,
And too much of earth for a dweller of heaven.
Yet the chain will burst and the bars be riven,
And the quest of my soul at last be given.
It shall stretch forth its wings and soar at last
From heav'n to heav'n in those realms vast;
It shall bask in the light of eternal truth,
And quench its thirst in the fountain of youth.

 * * * * * *

Hark! again mine ear drinks in a tone profound,
Like the far roar of ocean's liquid thunder,
Or voices of assembled storms remote—
So strangely, terribly, with life-sounds blent;
Yet musical and clear, that it would seem
The earth-encircling hymn of some strong angel's lyre;
While on its cadences sublime methinks I hear
The stirring sounds of martial strains or battle's yell:
As if the viewless heav'n-sent wanderer,
O'er fall'n myriads from Mars' red field,
Its cloud-clearing wings had swept.
'Twould seem, O eagle-winged winds of heaven,
Ye were the earth-directed harbingers of ill,
Unto a world guilt-stricken, from the great god of
 storms,

Who full of power rides in majestic wrath,
On chariot clouds, whose winged steeds
Are the embattling elements, lightning-reigned,
And full of speed—whose word is fate etern,
And his voice thunders.
                        Now madly shrieks
The spirit-voice along the arching sky,
Dying afar like peans o'er the slain.
   *   *   *   *   *

INDEX.

	PAGE.
Preface,	3
Memoirs of Mrs. L. A. H. Munday,	4
ACACIAN LYRICS,	7
Jerusalem,	7
Three Friends and the Jewel,	13
Stanzas for the Year,	16
Lines on the Death of Austin J. Morris,	18
An Allegory,	23
MISCELLANEOUS PIECES,	30
Reminiscences,	30
Lone Tree and Solitary Grave,	36
Song of the Genii,	38
Oceola's Lament,	42
Musings,	44
Rosseau's Heloise,	49
Autumn Winds are Sighing,	51
To a Young Poetess,	53
The Shipwreck,	56
The Graduate's Farewell,	58
The Moon,	60
To an Absent One,	62
To Leonore,	64
Music,	67
Lines on the Death of a Lady,	70
The Daguerrean Gallery,	74
The Pen,	75

INDEX.

Childhood's Rambles,	78
A Portrait,	83
Genius,	84
The Wandering Ship,	91
The Maniac,	94
My Native Land,	101
Musings,	103
To ——,	106
Paganini,	109
Epithelamium,	112
Lyrics,	113
SONGS OF WAR,	121
The Departure,	121
The March,	123
Rio Grande,	125
Palo Alto,	127
Notes to War Songs,	131
SONNETS AND SONGS,	133
Song of the Flowers,	133
Spring,	134
To a Friend,	135
Stanzas,	137
Isabel,	138
Written in a Lady's Album,	140
To a Portrait,	141
To ——,	141
Stanzas,	143
Song,	144
Stanzas,	145
Fantasies,	146
To Amanda Harte,	148
Song,	149
To Mary Bell,	151
Song,	152
A Dream of the Past,	152

The Serenade, - - - - 154
Song, - - - - - 155
ÆOLIAN MELODIES, - - - - 157
The Exiles Lament, - - - 159
The Broken Hearted, - - - 160
The Dying Boy, - - - 163
The Mother's Lament, - - - 164
The Orphans, - - - - 166
The Bereaved, - - - - 168
The Captive Chief, - - - 169
The Captive Exile, - - - 170
Euthanasia, - - - - 173
Sorrows of Genius, - ' - - 175

STANDARD AND VALUABLE

BOOKS,

Published and for Sale by

APPLEGATE & CO.,

BOOKSELLERS,
STATIONERS, PUBLISHERS, PRINTERS,
BINDERS AND BLANK BOOK
MANUFACTURERS.

43 MAIN STREET,
(BELOW SECOND)

CINCINNATI.

APPLEGATE & CO.'S PUBLICATIONS.

Dr. Adam Clarke's Commentary

On the Old and New Testaments.

With portrait of the Author engraved expressly for this edition accompanied with Maps, etc. Super-royal 8vo. sheep, spring back, marbled edge.

The Commentary of Dr. Clarke is most deservedly popular, being not only a truly scientific and elaborately learned work, but it is also well adapted to family reading. Liberal in his views, benevolent in his character Christian in his deportment, and deeply learned in Scripture lore, and all the science of the ancients as well as moderns, Dr. Clarke produced a work every way adapted to the wants of Bible students, preachers and families. This work, although the largest published west of the mountains, is yet afforded at a price within the reach of all.

"It would be difficult to find *any* contribution to Sacred Literature that has attained to a higher rank than the Commentaries of Dr. Adam Clarke. It is a treasury of knowledge, in the accumulation of which the author seems to have had no purpose in view but the apprehension of truth; not to sustain a particular creed, but the apprehension of truth for truth's own sake, restrained in the noble pursuits of no party tenets by no ardor for favorite dogmas."—*Nashville and Louisville Christian Advocate.*

"Of the merits of this work we need not speak, as its fame is as wide as the world of language in which it is written, and as imperishable as the name of its author; but of this edition we may say a word: It consists of four super-royal octavo volumes, two of the Old and two of the New Testament. The type is clear, printed upon a beautiful white paper, of superior texture, bound in a strong and substantial manner, with marbled edges. The first volume of the Old Testament contains a superior steel engraving of the author. The last volume contains the usual copious alphabetical index, while the entire work is embellished with the usual number of tables and maps. Upon the whole, this is an excellent and cheap edition of this great work of this great man."

"Much has been written in elucidation of its doctrines and precepts, by thousands of able authors, but there are none who have produced more simple and heart-touching expositions of the 'Book Divine,' or who have employed a greater fund of philological and biblical knowledge in the work than Dr. Adam Clarke."—*Christian Advocate.*

"This is a splendid super-royal edition of the commentary on the New Testament by that erudite and critical scholar, Dr. Adam Clarke. However persons may differ with Clarke in regard to his peculiar theological views, no one, we are assured, who is competent to form a judgment of his biblical and philological labors, will call in question his competency for the task he has performed, and we hesitate not to say that for laborious research no work of the kind has ever appeared, or perhaps ever will appear, exhibiting a more profound and extensive acquaintance with the whole range of Biblical literature. No theological student should be without this invaluable work. Henry and Scott, South, Doddridge and others, have furnished valuable practical commentaries, abounding with copious and luminous observations, but they are not EXPOSITIONS, such as the Bible student wants, and Clarke's Commentary stands unrivaled in this respect."—*Literary Casket.*

APPLEGATE & CO.'S PUBLICATIONS.

The Tattler and Guardian.

By ADDISON. STEELE, ETC., with an account of the authors, by Thos. Babbington Macaulay. Illustrated with steel plate engravings. Complete in one volume, with notes and general indexes.

TATTLER AND GUARDIAN.—*Addison* and *Steele* never wrote anything that was not good; but superlatively so is the Tattler and Guardian. In conjunction with the *Spectator*, (and neither of them is complete without the other) it affords a full view of English, as well as Continental Society, one hundred and fifty years ago, and in a quaint and classic style vividly portrays the follies and vices of the age. With pleasant humor, keen wit, and bitter sarcasm, it overflows, and is entirely free from the nonsense and commonplace twaddle and toadyism of much of the popular writings of the present day. It would be superfluous for us to say that the style in which it is written is chaste, classic and unique. No Library of Belles-Lettres is complete without it, and no scholar can appreciate the beauties of the English language until he has thoroughly studied the diction of Addison and Steele.

The splendid series of articles contained in these journals, having such authors as Addison. Steele and their associates, living through a century and a half, and still retaining all their freshness, can not but make them in their present shape sought after in every enlightened community.—*Cincinnati Daily Times.*

THE TATTLER AND GUARDIAN, whose capital Essays by Addison, Steele, Tickell and others, long since placed the volume in the foremost rank among the English classics.—*Cincinnati Press.*

They were and are yet models of composition, almost indispensable to a thorough knowledge of Belles-Lettres.—*Cincinnati Enquirer.*

The writings of Addison, Steele and their associates have rarely been issued in a form so well adapted for the general circulation which they deserve.—*Cincinnati Gazette.*

As a collection of rich essays, in beautiful English, The TATTLER needs no commendation from our pen.—*Ohio State Journal.*

The publishers have done the public a good service by placing this fountain of pure thought and pure English in a convenient form.—*Western Christian Advocate.*

No library is complete unless the TATTLER and GUARDIAN is on its shelves, and every man of literary tastes regards its possession as a necessity.—*Masonic Review.*

TATTLER AND GUARDIAN.—Who has not heard of Addison and Steele, and where is the scholar or lover of English Literature who has not read the Spectator? It is a part of English literature that we could not afford to lose. The writings of such men as Addison and Steele are good in any age. The book now before us is by the same authors.—*Ledger.*

Among all the flippant publications of the present day, in which there is an awful waste of paper and ink, it is refreshing to see a reprint of a work of standard merit such as the Tattler and Guardian. The criticisms of over a century have only more clearly pointed out its merits and established its reputation.—*Democrat.*

APPLEGATE & CO.'S PUBLICATIONS.

Mosheim's Ecclesiastical History;

Ancient and Modern, from the Birth of Christ to the beginning of the Eighteenth Century, in which the rise, progress and variations of Church Power are considered in their connection with the State of learning and philosophy, and the political history of Europe during that period. Continued to the year 1826, by Charles Coote, LL. D., 866 pages, quarto, sheep, spring back, marbled edge.

This edition forms the most splendid volume of Church History ever issued from the American Press; is printed with large type, on elegant paper, and altogether forms the most accessible and imposing history of the Church that is before the public.—*Gospel Herald.*

This great standard history of the Church from the birth of Christ, has just been issued in a new dress by the extensive publishing house of Applegate & Co. Nothing need be said by us in relation to the merits or reliability of Mosheim's History; it has long borne the approving seal of the Protestant world.—*Masonic Review.*

To the Christian world, next to the golden Bible itself, in value, is an accurate, faith'ul, and life-like delineation of the rise and progress, the development and decline of the Christian Church in all its varieties of sects and denominations, their tenets, doctrines, manners, customs and government. Such a work is Mosheim's Ecclesiastical History. Like "Rollin's History of the Ancients," it is the standard, and is too well known to need a word of comment.—*Advocate.*

But little need be said of the history as a standard work. It has stood first on the list of Church histories, from the day it became known to scholars, down to the present time; and there is but little probability that any new one will soon set it aside.—*Beauty of Holiness.*

No Church History, particularly as it respects the external part of it, was ever written, which was more full and reliable than this; and indeed, in all respects, we opine, it will be a long time before it will be superseded.—*Literary Casket.*

Who has not felt a desire to know something more of the early history, rise and progress of the Christian Church than can usually be found in the political histories of the world? Mosheim's Church History, just published by our Western Publishing House of Applegate & Co., contains just the information which every believer in Christianity so much needs. It fills the space hitherto void in Christian Literature, and furnishes a most valuable book for the student of Christianity. Every clergyman and teacher, every Sunday School and household, should have a copy of Mosheim's Church History.—*Herald.*

The work is printed on beautiful white paper, clear large type, and is bound in one handsome volume. No man ever sat down to read Mosheim in so pleasing a dress. What a treat is such an edition to one who has been studying the elegant work in the small, close print of other editions. Any one woh has not an ecclesiastical history should secure a copy of this edition. It is not necessary for us to say anything in relation to the merits of Mosheim's Church History. For judgment, taste, candor, moderation, simplicity, learning, accuracy, order, and comprehensiveness, it is unequaled. The author spared no pains to examine the original authors and "genuine sources of sacred history," and to scrutinize all the facts presented by the light of the "pure lamps of antiquity."—*Telescope, Dayton, O.*

APPLEGATE & CO.'S PUBLICATIONS.

Lorenzo Dow's Complete Works.

The Dealings of God, Man and the Devil, as exemplified in the Life, Experience and Travels of LORENZO DOW, in a period of over half a century, together with his Polemic and Miscellaneous Writings complete. To which is added, THE VICISSITUDES OF LIFE, by PEGGY DOW, with an Introductory Essay, by John Dowling, D. D., of New York, MAKING THE BEST AND MOST COMPLETE EDITION PUBLISHED. 1 vol. 8vo., library binding, spring back, marbled edge.

NOTICES OF THE PRESS.

Several editions of the Life and Works of Lorenzo Dow have been issued by different publishers, but the most complete and accurate is the one published by Applegate & Co., Cincinnati. After perusing it and reflecting on the good he accomplished not mentioned in this volume, we came to the conclusion that, if for the last hundred years, every minister had been a Lorenzo Dow, the whole world would have been civilized, if not christianized, some time since.

"No wonder that he was finally crucified at Georgetown, D. C., if it is true, as reported in some quarters, he was poisoned by some enemies who followed him to his retreat."

"Lorenzo Dow was not 'ONE,' but 'THREE' of them, a St. Paul in blessing souls—a Washington in seeking the best interests of his country, and a Howard in getting people 'out of the prison' of conservatism and oppression."

"We decide (*ex cathedra*) that one of the most interesting works ever placed on our table is 'The Complete Works of Lorenzo Dow,' embracing his travels in Europe and America, his polemic and poetical writings and 'Journey of Life,' by his wife Peggy, who heroically accompanied him in many of his peregrinations."

"Full as an egg is of meat, so was Lorenzo Dow of sparkling wit and genuine good humor. He overflowed with anecdote like a bubbling fountain in a sandy basin, and was never at a loss for a good and lively story wherewith to illustrate his subject and engage the attention of his hearers. His audience ever listened with breathless attention, and drank in his sayings with wondrous admiration and reverence. By some he was regarded as one of those special messengers the Almighty sent in times of great dearth of godliness and piety, to wake up the slumbering church. He evidently had his mission, and thousands now living throughout the land can testify as to how he filled it.

"His life was one continuous scene of adventure and anecdote, ever varying, and full of the life-giving power of enthusiasm. Spotless in purity, faultless in heart, and wholly devoted to the cause he had espoused—the cause of Christ."

"This is the best octavo edition of Dow's complete works now published. The writings of this remarkable and eccentric man have been before the public for years. They have been read by thousands. If not altogether unexceptionable, they embrace many wholesome truths. Vice in all its forms is rebuked with characteristic severity: his bitter sarcasm and cutting wit are employed in many instances to good effect. His wife seems to have been a kindred spirit, and both, with all their peculiar eccentricities, no doubt were truly devoted Christians, doing what they sincerely believed to be for the spiritual good of their fellow-beings, and the glory of God. Those who have not read this book will find sufficient to instruct and interest them."

APPLEGATE & CO.'S PUBLICATIONS.

Guizot's Gibbon's History of the Decline and Fall of the Roman Empire;

A new edition, revised and corrected throughout, preceded by a preface, and accompanied by notes, critical and historical, relating principally to the propagation of Christianity. By M. F. Guizot, Minister of Public Instruction for the kingdom of France. The Preface, Notes and Corrections translated from the French expressly for this edition—with a notice of the life and character of Gibbon, and Watson's reply to Gibbon. In 2 vols. imperial 8vo., sheep, spring back, marble edge.

We are pleased to see a republication of Guizot's Gibbon, with the notes, which have never before been republished in English. Gibbon, so far as we know, stands alone in filling up the historical space between the Roman Cæsars and the revival of literature.—*Cincinnati Chronicle.*

While there are numbers of Historians of the early days of the great Empire, Gibbon stands almost alone as the historian of its fall. The present edition, with the notes of Guizot, is a treasure of literature that will be highly prized.

The vices of the Roman Empire, that like the vipers in the bosom of Cleopatra, caused her destruction, are traced from their first inception, and should act as beacon-lights on the shores of time, to guide other nations that are following in her footsteps.

Altisonant Letters.

Letters from Squire Pedant in the East, to Lorenzo Altisonant, an emigrant to the West, for the Benefit of the Inquisitive Young. 1 vol. 12mo., cloth.

The publishers of the following letters do not present them as models of style, but as a pleasant means of obtaining the meaning of the greater part of the unusual words of the English language, on the principle of "association of ideas." In the column of a dictionary there is no connection between the definition of words, consequently, the committed definitions are soon lost to the pupil. By placing in such a juxtaposition as to form some kind of sense, the learner will the more readily retain the meaning of the word used

To the Youngsters. By the Author.

Young Friends:—Some one has said "that words not understood are like uncracked nuts—the lusciousness of the kernel is not enjoyed." Believing this to be so, and thinking that there are now many uncracked nuts in the English language, the author went up into old John Walker's garret, and gathered "lots" of old and hard nuts, and brought them down for you, and then he went into old Noah's ark—he means old Noah Webster's dictionary—and gathered many more, and by the assistance of Mr. Altisonant, placed them in the "letter basket," with the hammer, the dictionary, laid side by side. Will you take up the hammer and crack the nuts, and enjoy the kernel? Try it. Your friend, S. K. HOSHOUR.

A rare book this, and rare amusement it will afford to the reader.—*Daily Times.*

APPLEGATE & CO.'S PUBLICATIONS.

The Complete Works of Thos. Dick, LL. D.

11 vols. in 2; containing an Essay on the Improvement of Society; The Philosophy of a Future State; The Philosophy of Religion; The Mental Illumination and Moral Improvement of Mankind; An Essay on the Sins and Evils of Covetousness; The Christian Philosopher, or Science and Religion; Celestial Scenery Illustrated; Siderial Heavens planets, etc.; The Practical Astronomer; The Solar System, its wonders; The Atmosphere and Atmospherical Phenomena, etc. Illustrated with numerous engravings and a portrait. 2 vols. royal 8vo. sheep, spring back, marbled edge.

This edition is printed from entirely new plates, containing the recent revision of the author, and is the only COMPLETE edition published in the United States.

The works of Dr. Dick are so well known and appreciated, (being such as should be in the possession of every family and made the daily study of its members, old and young,) that the attempt to praise them would be like gilding fine gold.

"DICK'S WORKS.—Those who read at all, know both the name of Dr. Dick and the work itself, now reprinted. It has long found acceptance with the public."—*Presbyterian Review, Edinburgh.*

"The range of subjects contained in these several essays and scientific treatises is varied, all are highly important and of practical utility to mankind generally."—*Presbyterian of the West.*

"The best recommendation which can be given of Dr. Dick's Works is the great popularity they have enjoyed, and the numerous editions of them, collected and separate, which have been published in England and America. Messrs. Applegate & Co. are deserving of much praise for the tasteful and handsome style in which they have issued the work, and at such a price as to be within the reach of all."—*Cincinnati Gazette.*

"Dr. Dick's works have filled a place occupied by no others, and have presented the great facts of nature and the scientific movements and discoveries of the present age, in a manner at once both pleasing and instructive."—*Central Watchman.*

"The typography, plates, paper, and binding make the book more favorable in appearance than any publication we have yet seen in the West, and without exulting any, we are glad to say it equals the publications of like works in New York or Boston. How glad we are to see this, as it tells well for *go ahead* Ohio.—*Springfield Republic.*

"We hail this remarkably cheap and greatly improved edition of Dr. Dick's admirable and highly popular Works. It is a real boon to the millions to be able to purchase such an excellent work for so inconsiderable a cost. We earnestly recommend this work to all our readers, and especially to all who desire to store their minds with general information."—*Wesleyan Associate Magazine, London.*

Eleven different works are embraced in these volumes, making it an edition full and complete. The range of subjects embraced in these several essays and scientific treatises, is varied, all are highly important and of practical utility to mankind generally. These characteristics of Dr. Dick's writings, while they render them permanently valuable, insure for them also a wide circulation among all classes of readers.—*Presbyterian of the West.*

APPLEGATE & CO.'S PUBLICATIONS.

Plutarch's Lives,

With Historical and Critical Notes, and a LIFE OF PLUTARCH. Illustrated with a Portrait. 1 vol. royal 8vo., sheep, spring back, marbled edges.

This edition has been carefully revised and corrected, and is printed upon entirely new plates, stereotyped by ourselves, to correspond with our library edition of Dick, etc.

"Next in importance to a thorough knowledge of history, and in many respects fully equal to it, is the study of well authenticated biography. For this valuable purpose, we know of no work extant superior to the fifty lives of Plutarch. It is a rare magazine of literary and biographical knowledge. The eminent men whose lives compose this work, constitute almost the entire of that galaxy of greatness and brightness, which stretches across the horizon of the distant past, and casts upon the present time a mild and steady lustre. Many of them are among the most illustrious of the earth."—*Nashville and Louisville Christian Advocate.*

"No words of criticism, or of eulogy, need be spent on Plutarch's Lives. Every body knows it to be the most popular book of biographies now extant in any known language. It has been more read, by the youth of all nations, for the last four or five centuries in particular, than any ever written. It has done more good, in its way, and has been the means of forming more sublime resolutions, and even more sublime characters, than any other work with which we are acquainted, except the Bible. It is a better piece of property for a young man to own, than an eighty acre lot in the Mississippi Valley, or many hundred dollars in current money. We would rather leave it as a legacy to a son, had we to make the choice, than any moderate amount of property, if we were certain he would read it. There are probably but few really great men now living, that have not been largely indebted to it for their early aspirations, in consequence of which they have achieved their greatness."—*Ladies' Repository.*

"No book has been more generally sought after or read with greater avidity."—*Indiana State Sentinel.*

This is a magnificent 8vo., handsomely and substantially gotten up, in every respect highly creditable to the enterprising house of Applegate & Co. Who has not read Plutarch? for centuries it has occupied a commanding position in the literature of the age. It needs no eulogy; the reading public know it to be one of the most interesting, instructive and popular biographies now extant.—*St. Louis Republican.*

The Western public are under obligations to Messrs. Applegate & Co., of Cincinnati, for the handsome and substantial manner in which they have recently got up editions of several standard works. Dick's Works unabridged, Rollin's Ancient History, and now Plutarch's Lives, attest the enterprise and good judgment of this firm in their publishing department. To speak of the character and merits of Plutarch, which the old and the young of several generations are familiar with, would be presumptuous; but we can with propriety refer in terms of high commendation to the manner in which this edition has been got up in every department. The size is royal octavo, just right for the library. The paper is good, the typography excellent, and the calf binding just as it should be, neat and substantial. If this house continues as it has begun, it will soon have an extended and enviable reputation for the character and style of its editions of standard works, and it will deserve it.—*Cincinnati Daily Times.*

APPLEGATE & CO.'S PUBLICATIONS.

Rollin's Ancient History.

The Ancient History of the Carthagenians, Assyrians, Babylonians, Medes, and Persians, Grecians and Macedonians, including a History of the Arts and Sciences of the Ancients, with a Life of the Author. 2 vols. royal 8vo., sheep, spring back, marbled edge.

One of the most complete and impartial works ever published. It takes us back to early days, and makes us live and think with the men of by-gone centuries. It spreads out to us in a pleasant and interesting style, not only the events which characterize the early ages, but the inner world of thought and feeling, as it swayed the leading minds of the times. No library is complete without Rollin's Ancient History.

"A new edition of Rollin's Ancient History has just been issued by Applegate & Co. The value and importance of this work are universally acknowledged. Every private library is deficient without it; and it is now furnished at so cheap a rate, that every family should have it. It should be placed in the hands of all our youth, as infinitely more instructive and useful than the thousand and one trashy publications with which the country is deluged, and which are so apt to vitiate the taste and ruin the minds of young readers. One more word in behalf of this new edition of Rollin : It may not be generally known, that in previous English editions a large and interesting portion of the work has been suppressed. The deficiencies are here supplied and restored from the French editions, giving the copy of Messrs. Applegate & Co. a superiority over previous English editions."—*Western Recorder.*

"This work in this form has been for some years before the public, and is the best and most complete edition published. The work is comprised in two volumes of about six hundred pages each, containing the prefaces of Rollin and the 'History of the Arts and Sciences of the Ancients,' which have been omitted in most American editions."—*Springfield Republic.*

"The work is too well known, and has too long been a favorite to require any commendation from us. Though in some matters more recent investigations have led to conclusions different from those of the author, yet his general accuracy is unquestionable."— *Western Christian Advocate.*

"This work is so well known as standard—as necessary to the completion of every gentleman's library—that any extended notice of it would be folly on our part. We have named it for the purpose of calling the attention of our readers to the beautiful edition issued by the enterprising house of Mess. Applegate & Co "—*Methodist Protestant, Baltimore.*

The public are under obligations to Applegate & Co. for their splendid edition of this standard History.—*Times.*

Works like this, that form a connecting link between the splendid civilization of the ancients, and the more enduring progress of the moderns, are a boon to the lover of literature and the student of History.—*Railroad Record.*

Time is fleeting—Empires perish and monuments moulder. But a book like this survives the wreck of time and the ravages of decay.—*Globe.*

The history of departed kingdoms, with the causes of their sad decline and fall, serve as light-houses along the sea of life, to warn succeeding generations of their fate, and to teach them to avoid the rocks and quicksands of error and guilt on which they were wrecked. In no history is this purpose so well accomplished as in that of Rollin, a handsome edition of which has just been issued by Applegate & Co.—*News.*

APPLEGATE & CO.'S PUBLICATIONS.

The Spectator,

By ADDISON, STEELE, ETC., 1 vol. royal 8vo., 750 pages, with portrait of Addison. Sheep, spring back, marble edge.

The numerous calls for a COMPLETE and cheap edition of this valuable work, have induced us to *newly stereotype* it, in this form, corresponding in style and price with our other books. Its thorough revisions have been committed to competent hands, and will be found complete.

There is no work in the English language that has been more generally read, approved, and appreciated than THE SPECTATOR. It is a work that can be perused by persons of all classes and conditions of society with equal pleasure and profit.

"One hundred and forty years ago, when there were no daily newspapers nor periodicals, nor cheap fictions for the people, the Spectator had a daily circulation in England. It was witty, pithy, tasteful, and at times vigorous, and lashed the vices and follies of the age, and inculcated many useful lessons which would have been disregarded from more serious sources. It was widely popular."—*Central Christian Herald.*

"APPLEGATE & Co., 43 Main street, have just published, in a handsome octavo volume of 750 pages, one of the very best classics in our language. It would be superfluous at this day to write a line in commendation of this work."—*Cin. Com.*

"There are few works, if any, in the English language that have been more highly appreciated and generally read than the Spectator. It is in general circulation, and continues a popular work for general reading. The chaste style of its composition, and purity of its diction, has placed it high in rank among the English classics."—*St. Louis Republican.*

"It is a source of general satisfaction to hear of the republication of a work of such standard merit as the Spectator. In these days, when the press teems with the issue of ephemeral publications, to subserve the purpose of an hour, to enlist momentary attention, and leave no improvement on the mind, or impression on the heart—it is a cause of congratulation to see, now and then, coming from the press such works as this; to last as it should, so long as a pure taste is cultivated or esteemed."—*Cincinnati Gazette.*

"Criticism upon the literary merits of the Spectator would be rather late and superfluous at the present time. Steele, Addison and Swift are above criticism. This edition is gotten up in style and form that will make it peculiarly acceptable to the admirers of English literature. It is bound in one volume, with copious notes of the contributors prefixed. The type is clear and elegant, the paper good, and the binding excellently suitable for the library."—*Cincinnati Daily Times.*

"Amid the rush and whirl of this locomotive and high pressure age—amid the almost breathless rage for the light and flimsy effusions with which the laboring press is inundating the world, ADDISON, the immortal ADDISON,—one of the most beautiful, chaste, elegant, and instructive, as well as pleasing writers of the English language, may be pushed aside or overlooked for a time, but the healthful mind, satiated with the frothy productions of the times, will again return to such authors as Addison, and enjoy with renewed zest the pleasing converse of such pure and noble spirits."—*Methodist Monthly.*

www.ingramcontent.com/pod-product-compliance
Lightning Source LLC
Chambersburg PA
CBHW032226230426
43666CB00033B/1607